FOOTNOTE WASHINGTON

To Julie, Brennan, Julianne
In order of appearance.

Bryson B. Rash

FOOTNOTE WASHINGTON*

*Tracking the Engaging, Humorous and Surprising Bypaths of Capital History

EPM Publications, Inc.
McLean, Virginia

EPM Publications, Inc.
1003 Turkey Run Road
McLean, Virginia 22101
Printed in the United States of America

Book Design by Susan Lehmann
Illustrations © Betty Wells

Library of Congress Cataloging in Publication Data

Rash, Bryson B.
Footnote Washington.
1. Washington (D.C.)—Description—1981-
—Guide-books.   2. Washington (D.C.)—History.
I. Title.
F192.3.R37   1983   917.53'044   83-1572
ISBN 0-914440-62-4

Contents

Preface

Looking back, I think this book began with a story told by President Harry S Truman, an avid student of history who loved the small sidebar that adds spice and color to a person or event.

One day I was among a small group of reporters chatting with the President at the White House when the conversation turned to the Civil War. Mr. Truman regaled us with the story of the statue of General George H. Thomas in Thomas Circle in Washington, D.C. He related how the veterans of the Army of the Cumberland, who had raised the funds for the statue, gathered at the scene for the unveiling and dedication in 1879.

At the climactic moment the drape covering the statue was pulled aside. Instead of a great cheer a cry of disbelief arose from the throats of the Civil War veterans. General Thomas, the rock of Chickamauga, was astride a mare! Everyone who had ever served with him or saw him in the field knew that he rode only fiery stallions.

The clamor over the mistake, according to the President, was so great that the sculptor had to sneak back in the night and weld to the bronze horse the appropriate attachments.

It was years before I discovered that although the basic premise of the President's story was true, a few details were inaccurate. The dispute over whether the horse should be a mare or a stallion applied to the statue of General Winfield Scott, not General Thomas.

In any event, I repeated the story with relish many times to friends, and often they would have anecdotes of their own. Thus began my accumulation of the sidebars, the little known facts, the legends, the quirks of fate that give color and humor to history and people. My collection was added to by my deep-seated compulsion to read plaques and markers, or signs beside roads and on buildings.

I did not actively seek out anecdotes and vignettes, but over the years I accumulated a great number of them.

I have used some of this material in speeches and broadcasts, but never as a written collection of stories. Such use had not occurred to me.

After retiring in 1977 from NBC in Washington, I suggested to the then news director of WRC–TV, Bruce MacDonnell, that he occasionally include some of these stories as feature material in the station's regular television news broadcasts.

He was not at all interested. But I persisted.

One day, months later, Bruce asked if I thought I had enough material to sustain a one-hour television special. I assured him I did. He gave the go-ahead, and as I began in earnest to put the stories on paper and mold them for television, I realized the value of this kind of material.

After months of labor we developed a one-hour television program titled

"Washington Odyssey" made up almost entirely of the stories I had accumulated. It was broadcast on March 21, 1978. Throwing modesty to the winds, I can say that the program created an enormous impression and reaction. Even the *Washington Post* carried an editorial lauding the program not only for its content, but as an example of what could be done in the "cultural wasteland."

The original "Washington Odyssey" was rebroadcast several times. With material not included in the first program we produced several more half-hour versions, under the direction of David Nuell who had succeeded MacDonnell as news director of WRC–TV.

Early in 1979 the producers of the Washington version of the syndicated television program "P.M. Magazine" invited me to contribute to their program on WDVM–TV. I contributed stories for more than three years and the supply is still not exhausted.

During the production process of "Washington Odyssey" Bruce MacDonnell suggested I compile the stories in a book. I had little interest in that recommendation because I had no experience in writing for print or in getting a book published.

But over the past few years the idea of a book became more and more appealing. With the encouragement—the better word is nagging—of family and friends, I began work on these stories and found a publisher. This is the result.

This book is not intended to be a textbook, a historical treatise or a guidebook. Rather it is to make any kind of history more interesting and vital. I hope that the visitors and residents of the capital will see and *experience* the monuments and memorials, the streets and parks, the bronze and marble in human

The Washington Monument's first elevator was considered so dangerous that it was open only to men. Women and children had to climb the 897 steps to the top (see p. 53).

terms, as representative of living people who laughed and sorrowed, who achieved and who made mistakes. The city has many reminders of events large and small that shaped the nation and gave it strength, vitality and color.

Each of the stories is as factual as possible. Some have been embellished through inaccurate accounts by the observers or, over time, altered by dim memories or fanciful additions. Some are self-serving, others are sheer anecdote or legend. Some you will recognize, most you will not.

The purpose of the book is to inform and entertain.

The best reaction to any story I can hope for is "I didn't know that."

The Nation's Capital

During the Revolution the government of the colonies was a rather nomadic body. By 1783 the Continental Congress had settled comfortably in Philadelphia, and it looked as though the government would stay there for some time. One day a group of mutinous soldiers suddenly appeared and demanded their back pay. The demonstration so frightened the members of Congress that they moved posthaste to Princeton, New Jersey.

For this and other reasons it was imperative that a new city be built in a neutral location (preferably a virgin area) controlled by the federal, not state, government. Competition for the site of the capital began immediately, and the lobbying was fierce.

The argument narrowed down to two sites—the falls of the Delaware River near Trenton, New Jersey, and the Potomac River near Georgetown, with the former location preferred.

The question remained unresolved for years while the dispute became more and more bitter.

In 1787 the Congress assembled to revamp the Articles of Confederation and ended up adopting a whole new constitution. The debate over the location of a

Politics haven't changed much in nearly 200 years. Like many a deal, the one that placed the capital city in the south along the Potomac River was struck between two political adversaries.

federal city heated up. Vice President John Adams voted to locate it in Germantown, Pennsylvania.

As fate would have it, the "Assumption Bill" was defeated in Congress in early 1790. It was backed by Alexander Hamilton and would have provided for the federal government to assume the debts the states incurred fighting the Revolutionary War.

Thomas Jefferson, who represented Virginia, was the leader of the southern faction in the Congress that wanted the capital for its own.

A political deal based on a trade off was inevitable. Jefferson and Hamilton were political enemies, but the Virginian, seeing the opening, invited Hamilton to dinner. Also attending were several members of Congress from Virginia who had voted against the "Assumption Bill." As the evening progressed and the soft Madeira flowed, a bargain was struck. The Virginia congressmen agreed to change their vote against "assumption" if Hamilton would deliver sufficient northern votes to place the capital in the south—along the Potomac River. Politics haven't changed much in nearly 200 years.

Shortly after the dinner party both bills became law. President Washington was directed to choose the site, acquire the land and appoint building commissions for the new federal city.

That is how Washington, D.C., where it is today along the Potomac below the Little Falls, became the capital of the United States of America.

It was a political deal. Today we call it logrolling.

Capitol

Historian Allan Nevins wrote "the Capitol is the best loved and most revered building in America. It is history, the Major Symbol of the Nation, the spirit of America in stone."

It is all of that and more as it sits in brilliant, white, massive majesty on Capitol Hill.

☞ *The Missing Cornerstone*

The U.S. Capitol building as we know it today did not spring full-blown on the small hill above the malarial swamps along the Potomac. The architectural design was selected through a lengthy competition and many problems were overcome before construction began. By September 1793, the time had come to lay the cornerstone. On the 18th George Washington led a procession across the river from Virginia and through the woodlands of the new capital city. With bands playing and flags flying, uniformed militiamen and Masonic officials skirted the bog that was to become Pennsylvania Avenue and continued to Capitol Hill. There, wearing his Masonic apron, George Washington laid the cornerstone of the Capitol using a marble-headed gavel and a silver trowel. The ceremony ended in prayer and a volley of 15 rounds from the Alexandria Volunteer Artillery. The company then moved to what we would call a barbecue, with a 500-pound ox as the main dish.

The cornerstone George Washington laid on that day nearly 200 years ago was set into a silver plate marking the 13th year of American independence, the first year of Washington's second term as president and the year of Masonry 5793.

Today that cornerstone is missing. During the rebuilding of the East Front in the late 1950s no one could find it, even with metal detectors.

Usually cornerstone laying ceremonies are colorful public events with flags flying, martial music playing and leading figures orating. The festivities proclaim the importance of the occasion, the historic moment and the record of achievement left for future generations. It is all very impressive at the moment. But the fact is that memories are short, time blurs events and records are lost.

Today no one knows where the cornerstone of the Capitol is—but neither does anyone know precisely where the cornerstones of the White House, the Washington Monument and the Smithsonian Institution are located.

☞ *Freedom Statue*

The female figure crowning the cast-iron dome of the Capitol is not Pocahontas. It is a statue of *Freedom*. She is wearing a helmet with an eagle head and feathers, which is how the rumor started that the statue was of a Native American woman.

When the sculptor, Thomas Crawford, submitted his design, the man in charge of building the Capitol dome was Secretary of War Jefferson Davis, who later would become president of the Confederate States of America. In the original design for the *Freedom* statue that crossed Davis's desk, the figure wore the softly folded cloth liberty cap used by freed slaves in ancient Rome. Davis reacted violently. He suspected a Yankee abolitionist plot and would have nothing to do with anything that remotely suggested freed slaves.

Because the Secretary of War was the boss, the sculptor changed his design. That is why today *Freedom* looks slightly like an American Indian princess.

☞ *Rotunda Art*

The rotunda of the Capitol is one of the truly great rooms in America. It soars through unbroken space to measure 180 feet from the floor to the canopy of the dome. At the very top is Constantine Brumidi's painting, *The Apotheosis of George*

Washington, in which Washington is majestically seated, surrounded by 13 maidens symbolizing the original 13 states. Although this description of the figures is certainly the more acceptable one, those who know that Brumidi was a bon vivant and man-about-town believe the version of the story that claims that a number of the "maidens" look like some of the ladies of the evening whom the artist reportedly visited from time to time in Washington.

The huge paintings that hang on the walls of the rotunda include interesting details for those who want to find them. For example, in *Baptism of Pocahontas* by John Chapman, the Indian just behind the kneeling woman dressed in white has six toes on one foot.

● *The Embarkation of the Pilgrims* shows a sturdy, handsome Miles Standish kneeling in prayer; his left foot is enormous—perhaps a size 18 or 20 shoe. A man with a foot that big would have to be at least eight feet tall.

● *Declaration of Independence*, by John Trumbull, is also known as the "shin" picture. When the artist finished it, all the men seated in the front row had their legs crossed in the same direction and the most prominent feature was a row of stockinged shins. Trumbull fixed that by painting in a table or two.

☞ *Sculpture*

Some of the sculptures in the rotunda have their own intriguing stories as well.
● Lt. Uriah P. Levy of the United States Navy, a man of some means, was a

disciple of Thomas Jefferson. To express his love and devotion Levy commissioned one of France's finest artists to create a bronze likeness of the great statesman. Although the gift to the country was placed in the rotunda in 1834, Congress did not formally accept it. In the first half of the 19th century American tolerance for persons of a different race or religion was not high, and a gift from a man named Levy made members of the Congress uncomfortable. Within the year the statue was removed and placed on the north grounds of the White House. The executive branch of government, apparently, was less squeamish.

Forty years later, in 1874, the heirs of Lt. Uriah Levy demanded that the gift be formally accepted or returned. The Congress complied, and today the splendid statue of Thomas Jefferson stands in the rotunda of the Capitol.

• The statue of Lincoln was done by teenage sculptor Vinnie Ream. Because her congressman from Missouri represented her to the President as a poor young girl, Lincoln gave her permission to sketch him. For the last five months of Lincoln's life, Miss Ream spent frequent half-hour sessions in the President's White House office making sketches of him at work. The result was a bust, and later, on commission from Congress, the life-size statue of a pensive Abraham Lincoln in the rotunda.

• The head of Lincoln is by the famed sculptor Gutzon Borglum. In this work in the rotunda, in a similar one in the White House and in the monumental carving at Mount Rushmore, Borglum did not sculpt a left ear. He said that that incomplete image symbolized the unfinished life of Abraham Lincoln.

☞ *Statuary Hall*

National Statuary Hall in the U.S. Capitol holds a parade of the great men and women who shaped the United States. In 1864 Congress dedicated the old House of Representatives' chamber as a hall of fame in which each state had the privilege of placing marble or bronze statues of two of its heroes. By 1932 the collection had grown to 65 statues whose weight was causing the chamber floor to sag. The law was amended to limit states to one figure each. The remaining sculptures were moved to other prominent locations inside the Capitol.

John Gorrie of Florida is among Statuary Hall's great Americans, who include George Washington, Robert E. Lee, Henry Clay, Samuel Adams, Brigham Young, Sam Houston and Andrew Jackson. Gorrie is a very important man to 20th-century America.

A doctor of medicine, Gorrie's chief concern was the victims of malaria and other fevers in the steamy homes and hospitals of his native Florida. He worked unceasingly to alleviate their discomfort and, in the process, invented the artificial ice-making machine, and thus air conditioning. Gorrie's invention has made comfortable living possible on even the hottest days for people around the world. His machine also made possible the iced drink—the mint julep, the gin and tonic and anything else "on the rocks."

Ironically, the man responsible for all those ice cubes is just one figure removed in National Statuary Hall from Frances E. Willard of Illinois, who devoted her life and skills to the cause of temperance.

☞ *Bathtubs*

There were not many bathrooms in Washington in the first half of the 19th century, and it took a bit of arranging to get the use of a tub for bathing. About 1859, when the new Senate and House wings of the Capitol were finished, enormous bathtubs were installed in the basement for the convenience of the members. The bathtubs were of splendid marble imported from Italy, and were six feet or longer and quite deep. They were ideal for escaping the cares of the office and even helped ease the pain of congressmen suffering from hangovers. One of the tubs is still there, tucked away in the basement amid the pipes and machinery of the engineering department. It is, however, no longer used for bathing.

One story about the bathtubs that has come down through the years involves Henry Wilson, vice president in the Grant administration, who enjoyed the bathtubs and used them frequently. One day, according to legend, Wilson was called from the tub to his office on a matter of utmost urgency. Wrapping a towel around his wet body, he walked upstairs to his office. The exposure caused a "congestive chill" and a short while later Wilson died.

Some of the Senate guards swear that over the years they have occasionally heard coughing and sneezing and seen the dim figure of a person wrapped in a towel walking along the corridor leading to the office of the vice president.

☞ *Greenough's Washington*

Out of the mainstream of Capitol Hill tourist traffic on the second floor of the Smithsonian National Museum of American History is a neoclassical marble statue of a seated Lt. General George Washington. The statue is not hidden, but neither is it prominently displayed.

The 12-foot high, 12-ton statue rests in the Smithsonian after a disastrous sojourn at the Capitol where it was originally intended to be displayed.

As early as 1783, Congress authorized a statue to George Washington, but never appropriated the money for it. An attempt by Congress in 1800 to build a mausoleum failed when Washington's nephew refused to allow his uncle's body to leave Mount Vernon. Finally, on the centennial of Washington's birth, in 1832, Horatio Greenough was commissioned to sculpt a seated Washington.

The sculptor, an American, went to work immediately in his Florence, Italy, studio. Eight years later the statue was finished; then the problems began. The first obstacle was moving the gigantic sculpture from Florence to the port at Genoa for shipment to America. It took 22 yoke of oxen to pull the statue over the Italian roads. Some of the people who saw the statue pass thought it was a saint and properly kneeled and crossed themselves.

The Congress had sent a U.S. man-of-war to Genoa to bring the statue home, but because the statue was too big for the ship's hatches a merchant vessel was chartered.

A Congressional delegation met the ship when it arrived at the Navy Yard in Washington. The members of the delegation took one look at the statue and

were horrified to see that their great hero had been carved, seated in a chair, nude from the waist up. Virginia statesman General Henry A. Wise exclaimed, "The man does not live, and never did live, who saw Washington without his shirt."

It cost $5,000 to haul the statue from the Navy Yard to the Capitol rotunda, its designated place of honor. Because the marble Washington was too big for the doors at the rotunda entrance they were removed temporarily along with some of the masonry. Finally George Washington sat in neoclassical splendor in the rotunda of the Capitol building for all to admire.

Before long it was discovered that the statue was so heavy that the floor of the rotunda was beginning to sag. Congress directed that a pedestal be built on the floor below to support the statue.

The sculptor, Greenough, said he was dissatisfied with the statue's location in the rotunda because the light was bad, and the statue was moved to the west side of the building.

Just before the Civil War, George Washington was moved again, this time from the Capitol to an open area on the east plaza. Public ridicule then began in earnest, for there was the heroic likeness of the Father of the Country bare from the waist up, exposed to the elements. The bitter cold winds and rain swept the open plaza and in winter the snows clung to Washington's torso and drifted onto his lap. Noting Washington's outstretched sword, one wag said he was sure Washington was crying, "Take my sword if you will, but bring me some clothes."

For more than half a century George Washington endured these indignities until Congress finally gave up and, in 1908, turned the statue over to the Smithsonian Institution. The statue was placed in its present location in the National Museum of American History in 1963 while the building was under construction, because it was easier to build around the statue than to move it through doors and corridors.

One final indignity remains, however. While the statue resided on the Capitol's east plaza, it was placed on an enormous pedestal that could not be moved to the Smithsonian. The pedestal was used as the cornerstone for the power plant at E and South Capitol Streets, S.E., that supplies the Capitol. And there the pedestal sits today, boldly proclaiming to the world from the power plant: "First in War. First in Peace. First in the hearts of his countrymen."

☞ *Rare Books*

The Library of Congress houses the largest collection of books, manuscripts, music, photographs and other documents in the world. Tucked away in this vast array, mostly in the rare book division, are unusual specialized collections. For example, about 20,000 volumes of dime novels, some of which only cost a nickel when published, fill some shelves.

The Library of Congress's collection of the writings and documents of the great Hans Christian Andersen is the largest outside of his native Denmark. The screen actor Jean Hersholt and his wife made a gift of the collection "as a small token of the gratitude and love" they felt toward this country.

The late Harry Houdini, the world famous magician and student of the occult, once declared that over a period of 30 years he had read every single piece of literature on spiritualism that he could. He wrote, "I have collected one of the largest libraries in the world on psychic phenomenon, spiritualism, magic, witchcraft, demonology, and evil spirits." Houdini died in 1926 and bequeathed the principal part of his collection to the Library of Congress, along with a number of the mechanical objects he used in his magic shows.

The rare book division also houses a big collection of cookbooks called the

Katherine Golden Bitting Gastronomic Library. Among its treasures is the first cookbook ever published. The date was 1475, 17 years before Columbus landed in America; the title was *De honesta voluptate;* and the author was Bartolomeo Platina, who was also the Librarian of the Vatican. Among the recipes in this first cookbook is a very good version of ravioli. The recipe, loosely translated from the Latin by Leonard N. Beck, Curator of Special Collections, follows:

RAVIOLI IN TEMPO DE CARNE
(for ten guests)

Use half a pound of aged cheese and a little of some other fatty cheese, and a pound of the belly of a fat pork or veal.

Cook until well done; then blend with finely chopped aromatic herbs—pepper, ginger and clove. Adding the ground breast of a capon is a good idea.

Mix all these things together. Place the meat any way you like in well-ground meal.

These ravioli are not larger than a chestnut.

Cook them in a soup made of capon or some good meat. Place saffron on them when done.

They need to be boiled only as long as it takes to say two *Our Fathers*.

Serve on dishes and sprinkle with grated cheese and mild spices.

These ravioli can also be made from breast of pheasant or partridge or other fowl.

☞ *Sewall-Belmont House*

Just a block or so from the Library of Congress is a museum and research center dedicated to the cause of equality of rights for women. It is in the historic Sewall-Belmont House at 2nd Street and Constitution Avenue, N.E. Now the headquarters of the National Woman's Party, it houses the mementos of the heroines of the equality movement, among them Lucretia Mott, Susan B. Anthony and Alice Paul, who wrote the Equal Rights Amendment.

Aside from its significance to the women's movement, the Sewall-Belmont House has its own historic value. An early secretary of the treasury, Albert Gallatin, rented the house during his term in office, and, because no building for his government department was available, used the home as an office. It was in the living room of the Sewall-Belmont House that he worked out the financial details of the $15 million Louisiana Purchase in 1803, one of the more important events in the development of the nation.

☞ *Navy Yard*

Not far from the Capitol, at 9th and I Streets, S.E., is the U.S. Marine Corps Barracks. Thomas Jefferson selected this site as a place to quarter elite troops to protect the Congress and the nearby Washington Navy Yard, if necessary.

The oldest naval installation in America, the Yard was established in 1799 in an area along the Anacostia River that George Washington selected. In the beginning ships for the Navy were built here. Later the Yard became the principal source for naval armaments and munitions. The big 14- and 16-inch guns used aboard the battleships of the 20th-century U.S. Navy were manufactured in the massive industrial complex of the Yard.

The Yard also houses the U.S. Navy Memorial Museum filled with guns of all sizes and descriptions; the hut used by Admiral Richard Byrd at the South Pole; replicas of the A bombs dropped on Hiroshima and Nagasaki; and the deepest-diving submersible in the world, the *Trieste*.

☞ *Intelligent Whale*

An annex next to the U.S. Navy Memorial Museum houses a two-man German miniature submarine, a Japanese manned suicide torpedo and a cigar-shaped, ungainly object called the *Intelligent Whale*—an early, experimental submarine.

The *Whale* was built in Newark, New Jersey, sometime between 1864 and 1872 by a General Hoxey, who had a terrible time finding a crew to man his vessel when it was ready for testing. No one in his right mind was willing to get inside the iron object, sail it away from dock and sink it. Finally, a General Sweeney got together a crew of men willing to take the risk. (How two generals got into an experiment involving a Navy vessel is an unknown footnote in history.)

In any event, the fearless crew took the *Whale* out in New York harbor and dived it to 16 feet. Motive power was supplied by six crewmen furiously turning a long handcrank inside the sub that ran an exterior screw. Top speed submerged was four knots.

As the submarine approached the test target, which was a scow anchored in the estuary, General Sweeney put on a diver's suit. Through a manhole in the vessel's underbelly (the only way in or out of the *Whale)* Sweeney made his way underwater to the target, attached a torpedo or mine to the hull of the scow and got back inside the submarine.

The crew frantically turned the handcrank to get away from the explosion that moments later blew the target to pieces. No one really knows how Sweeney fired the explosive, but presumably he did it with a lanyard attached to the outside of the submarine. As the *Whale* moved away, the trigger was pulled.

Fortunately Sweeney and the entire crew survived, but the Navy abandoned the whole idea until about 1900 when the submarine service was established.

☞ *Dahlgren's Leg*

Admiral John Dahlgren is one of the legendary officers in the history of the United States Navy. He commanded the Navy Yard in Washington during the Civil War. Among other things, he invented the famous Dahlgren naval gun.

He is remembered by the hall named for him at the U.S. Naval Academy in Annapolis, by a weapons proving ground in Virginia and by one of the most bizarre ceremonies that has ever taken place in Washington.

Admiral Dahlgren had a son, Ulric, who was an ambitious, young Union Army officer. As Robert E. Lee and the Confederate Army retreated after the battle of Gettysburg, Ulric Dahlgren was ordered to harass the rebel forces.

In a fierce running battle in the streets of Hagerstown, Maryland, young Dahlgren was wounded. He was brought back to Washington by ambulance. The best doctors in the Capital concluded that the only way to save the young officer's life was to amputate his leg. After the operation Admiral Dahlgren took possession of the severed limb. He knew exactly what he wanted to do with it.

The next day Colonel Ulric Dahlgren's severed leg, wrapped in an American flag and resting in a small box, was brought to the Navy Yard. It was met at the portal by a Marine detachment and with full military honors was taken to a new foundry being built by Admiral Dahlgren. There, in a solemn ceremony, Colonel Dahlgren's leg was placed in the wall.

And to this day a plaque on the foundry wall commemorates the heroism of Colonel Dahlgren and the interment of his lost leg.

White House and Vicinity

The White House sits in serene, simple beauty in its small, green, tree-shaded park in the heart of downtown Washington. The White House is a museum of American history and part of every American's national heritage. It is the home and the office of the only person elected by all the people to represent them and to be directly accountable to them.

The center of a vast communications and work complex, the White House contains all of the modern technology necessary to operate a massive government.

The mansion also offers all the amenities needed to provide comfort and security to the president and his family. Over the years the house has reflected the various technological advances and standards of living as they have changed with time.

● Water for the indoor "water closets" used during the time of Jefferson and for the rest of the house was supplied from cisterns located on the roof. Running water from outside the mansion was not available until the time of President Jackson in 1834. The water was piped in from springs in Franklin Park about seven blocks away at 14th and I Streets, N.W.

- A payment of $25 for an "icebox" was authorized in 1845.
- Gas lights were installed in 1849.
- Until 1853 the mansion was heated by fireplaces, and the number of cords of wood used was astronomical. President Franklin Pierce enjoyed not only the first central heating plant, but also the first genuine bathroom.
- Alexander Graham Bell's new invention, the telephone, was installed in the White House in 1877. One story has it that President Rutherford B. Hayes was fond of calling an official at the Treasury Department across the street who would entertain the chief executive by singing operatic arias on the new instrument.
- Another new invention came to the White House in 1891 when electric lights replaced the gas lights.
- The first president to ride in an automobile was Teddy Roosevelt. That occurred before he occupied the White House. It wasn't until 1921 that Warren G. Harding became the first president to ride to his inaugural in the horseless carriage.
- Air-conditioning units were placed in some bedrooms in 1935. The mansion was not cooled from a central unit until years later.
- At small private affairs in the White House President Harry S Truman* would

---

* President Truman's middle initial S is not followed by a period to denote an abbreviation. He had no middle name, and the letter S was adopted because it stood for each of his grandfathers: Anderson Shippe Truman and Solomon Young. Later President Truman preferred the name Shippe, but since it was never formally adopted or used the initial has no particular significance.

joke that anyone who wanted a cocktail before dinner would find the makings in the closet. But there weren't any closets in the White House until 1952, when the massive rebuilding by the Truman administration was completed.

☞ *Stuart Painting*

The East Room of the White House was originally designed by architect James Hoban as the residence's "public audience room" and was intended to be the most elegant of the state reception rooms. It has had other functions too: it was there that Abigail Adams dried the laundry. The room was almost ruined by the rowdies who attended Andrew Jackson's inaugural. It has also been the scene of weddings, dances, receptions, funerals and news conferences, and it has endured a myriad of decorative schemes.

The only object now in the East Room that was there when the room was finished in 1800 is the Gilbert Stuart full-length portrait of George Washington. But even the portrait might not have survived if Dolley Madison had not risked capture by waiting to have it removed as British troops advanced to burn the capital in 1814.

The Washington portrait is one of several copies made by Gilbert Stuart of his original *Lansdowne* painting which was commissioned by Senator William Bingham of Pennsylvania in 1796. Because there was no way to mechanically reproduce a painting in those days before photography, the artist made a number of copies for sale to make a profit. But Stuart may have been in a hurry when he made this copy. One of the two books leaning against the leg of the table near Washington is the *Constitution and Laws of the United States*. In his haste or forgetfulness, though, Stuart misspelled a word: the title of the book in the White House portrait is the *Constitution and Laws of the United Sates*.

☞ *Front Door*

The north entrance, at 1600 Pennsylvania Avenue, with its graceful columns and portico is the one depicted in photographs and on film and videotape as the front door of the White House. But it wasn't always that way.

In the beginning the whole area was called, simply, President's Park. Pennsylvania Avenue was not cut through until 1840, and the present system of addresses in Washington was not used until 1870. It is probable that the White House didn't get the 1600 Pennsylvania Avenue address until the 1920s.

President John Adams, the residence's first tenant, used the south portico with its porches and stairways as the front door because it offered a spectacular view of the broad Potomac and the low Virginia hills. Another reason Adams used the south entrance was that the north side lacked a portico until 1829. Up to that time the entrance section was flat with four columns supporting a pedi-

Entrance on the south lawn of the White House.

ment containing an American eagle. A short staircase rose from the ground to the door.

Today both entrances are used, but for different purposes. Most guests still enter the White House from the south side through the diplomatic reception room. With rare exceptions, only heads of states or governments enter the White House through the north portico; it is the ceremonial entrance.

In any event, architect James Hoban planned the north portico as the front door; so, history and precedent notwithstanding, that's the front door.

☞ *F.D.R. Bomb Shelter*

After the United States entered World War II, Washingtonians lived in deathly fear of an enemy air attack. German airpower had been instrumental in crushing Poland and the allied armies in the West, and Japanese navy planes had all but destroyed the U.S. fleet at Pearl Harbor.

At the center of the fear was the safety of President Franklin D. Roosevelt who worked and lived in that inviting target, the White House. So, within days after December 7, 1941, earth-moving equipment began tearing at the east lawn to build a deep tunnel to the Treasury Department.

One of the Treasury's safest vaults, 30 feet below Pennsylvania Avenue, was cleared of the valuables it held and refurbished as a bomb-proof shelter for the President who, in the event of an air attack, would be whisked from the White House through the tunnel under the east lawn and into the bowels of the Treasury Department to safety.

Although the shelter was sparsely furnished because it was only an interim stopping place, it was equipped with elaborate communications facilities. A few blocks south of the White House, a special railroad car stood on the tracks at the Bureau of Engraving and Printing and, when the air attack had ended, the President would be quickly taken out of the city to a safe location.

The shelter was never used, but it is still there and available. Under a nuclear attack today it would be useless, however.

That tunnel from the White House to the bomb shelter still serves as a useful avenue of privacy in the fishbowl of Washington because there is also a tunnel under Pennsylvania Avenue to the Treasury annex across the street and a connecting alley from that building to H Street. So it is possible to go in or out of the White House to a handy location a block or so away without being seen.

☞ *Settlers' Memorial*

In the Ellipse or President's Park, just south of the White House is a small granite shaft that few people walking by on 15th Street ever notice. But this memorial is important to an understanding of the nation's capital.

The memorial is dedicated to the 18 landowners whose property eventually became Washington, D.C. Their names are cut into the granite, and the four panels on the shaft symbolize the agricultural pursuits—corn and tobacco—and the bounty of game and fish—wild turkey and herring—that sustained the early settlers.

☞ *MacArthur's Planters*

There is no great memorial in Washington to General Douglas MacArthur. However, there is one small reminder of the World War II army hero and gover-

nor of Japan after the surrender. The memorial is so commonplace that very few people even notice it.

For a very short time in 1916, then Captain Douglas MacArthur was superintendent of the State, War and Navy Department building, which is now the old Executive Office Building next to the White House.

To brighten up the enormous bulk of the building, MacArthur installed precisely parallel rows of stone planters leading from the north steps to Pennsylvania Avenue to hold flowers and ornamental shrubs.

And there they are today, MacArthur's planters, the single reminder of him in the capital other than a boulevard re-named for the flamboyant general.

☞ *Dan Sickles's Leg*

In a plexiglass exhibit box in the Armed Forces Medical Museum on the grounds of Walter Reed Army Medical Center is a shattered leg bone. Beside it is the cannonball that did the damage. This is the remains of the amputated leg of one of the most irascible characters Washington has ever known.

Daniel Sickles was a former Tammany Hall congressman in 1854 when he married a vivacious 17-year-old Italian girl named Theresa. When he returned in 1856 with his wife from a diplomatic assignment in London and regained his old seat in Congress, his home on Lafayette Square became a swirling center of social activity.

At one of the soirees Theresa met the dashing Philip Barton Key, son of the composer of the national anthem and a district attorney for Washington. Before long their flirtation blossomed into a torrid affair. Key acquired an apartment just a block or so from the Sickleses' house and it was there the liaison flourished. When Key wished to see his beloved he would walk by her home and wave his handkerchief; she would join him shortly thereafter.

As fate would have it, someone sent Sickles an anonymous note telling him of the "notorious affair" and giving the congressman the address of the apartment. He confronted Theresa with this information and she confessed. Sickles was distraught, and on a Sunday afternoon in 1859, he watched from his window as Key walked by and flicked his handkerchief to signal a meeting with Theresa. Sickles rushed from his home on Lafayette Square with two pistols and shot and killed his wife's lover.

In the sensational trial for murder that followed, Sickles was acquitted. It was the first time a plea of temporary insanity was used in a U.S. court. The juicy scandal also resulted in divorce for the Sickleses.

When the Civil War erupted a few years later, Sickles raised a body of troops and received an officer's commission. By the time of the Battle of Gettysburg, Sickles had been made a major general in command of an army corps. He nearly lost the engagement at Gettysburg for the union forces, however. He was in charge of the left side of the union line, and, without orders and without notifying Commanding General George C. Meade, Sickles advanced his forces. His corps was cut to pieces by confederate General Longstreet's attack in the Peach Orchard and the Wheat Field at Gettysburg. Sickles's right leg was

torn off by a cannonball in the swirling, confused battle. In his usual flamboyant manner Sickles brought the severed limb and the cannonball back with him to Washington as a donation to the army's medical museum.

Meade was so angry with Sickles for advancing at Gettysburg that he wanted Sickles court-martialed. Nothing came of the court-martial attempt, however, because of the grievous wound the Major General had suffered, and because of the friends he had in high places.

There is one more footnote to the odyssey of Dan Sickles. After the war President Grant appointed him minister to Spain where he reportedly became the lover of the Queen and, to hush up a scandal, married one of her ladies-in-waiting.

No J Street

The alphabetical listing of Washington's east-west streets contains no *J* street. There are a number of reasons for this historic slight to a noble letter.

One reason is that, for centuries, the letters *I* and *J* were interchangeable. The monks who illuminated early manuscripts drew the two capital letters in almost identical fashion. In fact, the letter *J* did not become a universally recognized part of the (English) alphabet until relatively recently, perhaps as late as 1700.

Also, those who were illiterate (and that included many of the early population of Washington) were confused by oral directions that distinguished between the letters *J* and *K*.

The more amusing but unfounded story that explains why there is no *J* street in Washington maintains that the original city planner, Major Pierre L'Enfant, intensely disliked Chief Justice John Jay and deliberately left out the letter *J* as a slight to that worthy man.

Northwest Washington has no *B* street. Originally there was one, but it was obliterated when a canal was dug through the heart of the downtown area. The canal was filled in and paved over in the late 1800s. *B* street was renamed Constitution Avenue in 1931.

Washington Monument

The Washington Monument is the most visually striking landmark in the nation's capital. It took more than a hundred years and countless designs before the now familiar obelisk was completed.

The story of the Washington Monument began in 1783 when the Continental Congress passed a resolution providing for an "equestrian statue of General Washington." Eight years later L'Enfant made a place for it in his plan of the city, but because President Washington objected to the struggling nation spending money on the statue the proposal was dropped.

Over the years, several ideas for a monument to the nation's first president were proposed and forgotten, including a marble tomb, a crypt in the Capitol and a monument in the city. In 1833 a group of prominent citizens formed the Washington Monument Society and began soliciting $1 contributions. In seven years, however, less than $30,000 was collected. Nevertheless, in 1848 Congress finally approved the site for the monument, and with much fanfare the cornerstone was laid on the Fourth of July.

In its early days the Washington Monument Society also solicited funds from each state in the union to supplement individual contributions. Because Alabama didn't have money it sent a stone instead. The Society quickly adopted this idea, and soon more than a hundred stones had been gathered together in the work yards around the base of the monument. Then, as a Washington newspaper reported, "a deed of barbarism was enacted." The "deed" involved the stone given by Pope Pius IX and a splinter political party called the Know Nothings, whose members were violently anti-Catholic. The Know Nothings had vowed that the "Pope's stone," as it had come to be known, would never become part of the Washington Monument.

On the night of March 6, 1854, between 1:00 and 2:00 A.M. a group of four to ten men rushed out of the darkness and surrounded the shack of the night watchman hired to guard the monument and the gift stones. The men imprisoned the watchman and stole the Pope's stone from the lapidarium on the grounds and trundled it off in a handcart. It was believed that the stone was taken to the Potomac a few hundred yards away and dumped into the water near what is now the 14th Street bridge. The stone has never been found and the perpetrators were never brought to justice.

There is a bit more to the story: the night watchman could neither explain why he waited almost two hours after the assault before sounding the alarm nor why he failed to use his double-barreled shotgun to drive off the intruders. He was fired by the Washington Monument Society, and, to this day, he is suspected of being a member of the Know Nothing party and a conspirator in the plot to prevent the Pope's stone from being part of the monument to the first president.

On November 16, 1982, Father James E. Grant of the Catholic diocese of

Spokane, Washington, presented a replica of the original Pope's stone to the National Park Service for the Washington Monument. Made of Italian carrara marble, its Latin inscription reads "From Rome to America." The new stone has been placed in an appropriate location on the interior wall of the monument.

Another gift stone is missing. France sent one from the tomb of Napoleon the Great. It was last seen in the Brooklyn Navy Yard in 1861, and has not yet been found.

Almost 200 other memorial stones are set into the monument's interior walls. These stones were given by foreign governments, states, cities, fraternal and patriotic organizations and temperance groups. (The one from China praised President Washington in Chinese.) The Cherokee Nation is represented. The stone from Arizona contains three pieces of petrified wood. Nineteen cities, 20 Masonic Lodges, 14 Oddfellow Lodges and 7 divisions of Sons of Temperance are represented. There are also a mosaic block from the ruins of Carthage; lava from Vesuvius; and a stone each from the chapel of William Tell in Luzerne, Switzerland; the Ladies and Gentlemen, Dramatic Profession of America; and the 1857 American residents of Foo-Chow-Foo, China.

With the stones and public contributions, work on the monument continued until the Civil War diverted the nation's attention. Construction came to a halt at 150 feet. The square stub of marble remained for 15 years until Congress appropriated $200,000 in 1876 to finish the monument.

An examination of the substructure before construction resumed revealed that the footing was inadequate and the monument had tilted from the vertical.

A new 13½-foot slab of concrete was put under the base and the monument righted. Then the designers couldn't match the original marble, which accounts for the differing tints of the shaft.

Finally, the monument was opened to the public on October 9, 1888. The steam elevator that carried passengers to the top was considered so dangerous that only men were permitted to use it. The hazardous ride was eased, though, because the lift's male passengers were served cheese, wine and beer during the time-consuming trip up and down. Meanwhile, women and children had to make the exhausting climb up the 897 steps to the top and back down again on foot.

When the stairway was closed in the 1960s because of vandalism and occasional injury to some who ventured too close to the wire-enclosed elevator shaft, one of the more interesting walking tours in Washington—the memorial stones inside the Washington Monument—was ended.

The Washington Monument is not in the place originally selected for it—the exact center of the land area of the new federal city, which then included Arlington County, Virginia. To mark the original site a few hundred feet from the present location, Thomas Jefferson laid a pier stone. That stone slowly sank in the marshland along the bank of the Potomac until it disappeared entirely. It was later recovered and placed on the present monument grounds. Strangely enough, the pier stone bears an obvious resemblance to the present structure despite the fact that Jefferson's marker was designed more than half a century before the final form of the Washington Monument was decided upon.

Also on the grounds of the monument is a manhole cover that, when lifted, reveals a miniature Washington Monument set into the ground. This is a measuring device used to calculate the stability of the 555-foot-tall marble obelisk. A few years ago it was reported that the monument was sinking at a rate of ¼ inch to ½ inch each year. This meant that ultimately the monument would disappear. Today, however, the ground under the structure has compacted and the sinking has stopped; the danger is over.

Postscript

Willard Scott, the well-known television weatherman and Washington history buff, found a story in an old almanac on how the problem of continuing construction on the Washington Monument was overcome. He believes it, but there is little supporting evidence. According to the story, the engineers were stymied about how to maneuver a line up over the monument walls so they could scale the walls to inspect the work without building an expensive and perhaps unnecessary scaffold. One engineer hit on a brilliant idea: a pigeon with a string tied around its foot would be released inside the structure and would carry the line up and over the wall to the outside. The terrified bird quickly flew to the open top and outside to freedom. Hired sharpshooters stationed around the monument shot the pigeon down when it emerged. The string around its foot was the beginning of the line which, when extended with heavier and heavier cord and rope, made it possible to continue building the monument.

Lincoln Memorial

One of the most majestic and hallowed shrines in Washington is the Lincoln Memorial—a Greek temple sitting on the Potomac shore. The statue inside is perhaps the best known piece of sculpture in the United States. It portrays the great Civil War president sitting in repose with his arms extended and resting on the chair. Most who have seen the sculpture agree that the artist caught the strength and humanitarianism of the martyred president.

Shortly before the sculptor Daniel Chester French made this statue of Lincoln, he created the memorial to Thomas Hopkins Gallaudet, the pioneer educator of the deaf. The statue shows Gallaudet teaching sign language to his first deaf student.

French was so touched by Gallaudet and his work that when he created the Lincoln statue he shaped the President's left hand in the sign language equivalent of the letter *A* and his right hand in a modified letter *L*.

It was Lincoln who signed the bill that chartered Gallaudet College for the deaf.

Incidentally, football's first huddle was held at Gallaudet College to enable the deaf students to use sign language to communicate their plays to team members without being seen by the opposing team. The football players gathered in a closed circle, a huddle, to conceal their intentions.

☞ *Gunfire*

Only one building in Washington was hit by gunfire during all of World War II, and the enemy didn't do it.

During the war government officials in the nation's capital were obsessed by the fear of an aerial attack on the city. So, immediately after the attack on Pearl Harbor, they ordered anti-aircraft guns set up around Washington, and many were mounted on public and private buildings. Although several of the guns were dummies put in place to show the enemy and its spies that the city was prepared to defend itself, one very real gun was mounted on the roof of the Department of the Interior building at 18th and C Streets, N.W., where on pleasant days many government workers took their breaks while enjoying the open air and the spectacular view.

One bright day an unnamed employee walked over to the bored gun crew of the anti-aircraft weapon. Perhaps it was a member of the crew or the employee who did it, but in any event the sighting gears that adjusted the muzzle on the weapon were twirled and the lanyard absentmindedly pulled. With a roar the gun fired. The target was the Lincoln Memorial just a few blocks away. One projectile hit the top level of the memorial and knocked a large chunk of marble out of the panel that bore the seal of the state of Maryland. Other projectiles hit near Texas and Connecticut. The holes have been patched, but you can still see the bullet marks if you look closely.

☞ *Cherry Blossoms*

One of the picture-postcard images of Washington, along with the Lincoln and Jefferson Memorials and the Washington Monument, is the delicate beauty of the Japanese cherry blossoms. Now the trees form a pale pink fringe along the river and the tidal basin. But they have had their bad moments.

When the first shipment of trees arrived in Washington from Tokyo in 1909, hard-eyed inspectors from the Department of Agriculture took one look at the trees and ordered them destroyed. They were infested with insects and had fungus disease.

Although Japan and the United States were on very friendly terms, the incident created a major diplomatic problem which was solved by gently suggesting to the Japanese ambassador that the city of Tokyo, the original donor, send other trees after taking the necessary steps to disinfect them.

The new consignment arrived in early 1912. In a simple ceremony the then first lady Mrs. William Howard Taft and the wife of the Japanese ambassador planted the first trees. They are still there along the Potomac near the Lincoln Memorial and are marked by an appropriate plaque.

When the Jefferson Memorial was built, some of the cherry trees had to be removed. Women crusaders protested vehemently, and some of the more militant demonstrators chained themselves to trees while others sat in the holes left by trees that had been removed. The protest subsided when it was pointed out that an additional thousand trees were to be planted when the Memorial was finished.

The worst case of vandalism to the trees occurred in the first few days after the Japanese attack on Pearl Harbor; three or four of the trees were cut down in retaliation.

☞ *Foggy Bottom*

The memorial to the martyred Abraham Lincoln went through the same decades of travail that preceded the building of the Washington Monument. The effort began in 1867 when Congress authorized tentative plans to be drawn. Nothing came of those plans until 1911 when Congress created the Lincoln Memorial Commission with former President William Howard Taft as chairman.

The commission selected the site where the Lincoln Memorial stands today. The choice created an uproar because the site was a malarial swamp with scattered marshy pools and no access by bridge or road.

House Speaker Joe Cannon warned at the time that "malarial ague from the mosquitoes of the swamp would shake the memorial to pieces." But the work went forward. Enormous piles were driven into the muck of "foggy bottom" to support the white marble temple. Today stalagmites and stalactites abound in the huge man-made concrete chamber under the memorial.

The area north and west of the memorial has its own history. In 1768 a German immigrant named Jacob Funk bought a 130-acre tract along the Potomac at Rock Creek that consisted of swampland and one high hill. He laid out a town that he called Hamburg and hoped it would rival Georgetown as a center for busy river and seaport traffic.

In a rough outline for the new federal city, Thomas Jefferson, who admired Funk's land, wrote, "the highest summit of the land in the town heretofore called Hamburg shall be appropriated for a capitol for the accommodation of Congress." However, Major Pierre L'Enfant, who laid out the city, preferred another spot called Jenkins Hill about a mile away. George Washington approved L'Enfant's design and the Capitol stands on Jenkins Hill instead of on the hill in the town of Hamburg in Foggy Bottom.

Funk's and Jefferson's hope for Hamburg failed, and the area deteriorated. But later, although Hamburg didn't get the Capitol, it got the State Department.

While foreign affairs are conducted for Great Britain at Whitehall, a section of London near the Thames, and for France at the Quai d'Orsay, a street along the Seine in Paris, foreign affairs for the United States are conducted in Foggy Bottom, a one time miasmic swamp along the Potomac.

☞ Old Naval Observatory

Boundary is a simple word meaning a separating line. Questions about boundaries have resulted in law suits, fist fights, shootings, and, when they involve nations, war. For more than 100 years the central point from which boundaries were reckoned for the United States was in Washington. The original meridian was in the middle of what is now 16th Street just north of Florida Avenue.

In 1850 Congress established the Washington meridian at the center of the dome of the old Naval Observatory, which is now the headquarters of the Naval Medical Command at 23rd and E Streets, N.W. The boundaries of most of the western and plains states—Arizona, Colorado, the Dakotas, Idaho, Montana, Wyoming, Kansas, Nebraska, New Mexico and Utah—were drawn from that precise point.

By the way, just across the road from the old Naval Observatory is the statue of Dr. Benjamin Rush. He was a leading patriot of the Revolution and an outstanding physician. A signer of the Declaration of Independence, Rush was also surgeon-general of the Revolutionary Army for a time.

Dr. Rush opened the nation's first public health clinic in Philadelphia in 1786. He was far ahead of his times in his approach to social issues. Rush advocated temperance, education for women and abolition of public and capital punishment.

And, Dr. Benjamin Rush was also America's first alienist—that is, psychiatrist.

☞ *Braddock's Rock*

There are a lot of strange plaques and unusual memorials in Washington to now unknown people and events. Braddock's Rock, though, is perhaps the most unusual of all Washington's memorials, because it is at the bottom of a well shaft protected by a steel manhole cover. The well shaft was dug when the approaches to the Theodore Roosevelt Bridge were built.

In the early 18th century the Maryland shore of the Potomac along what is now northwest Washington was a marshy swampland, and the only solid ground was a large outcropping of rock just south of where Rock Creek empties into the Potomac. In 1755 British Major General Edward Braddock, with then Lt. Colonel George Washington at his side, moved his troops across the Potomac from Virginia and landed them on the outcropping of rock on the Maryland side. It was the beginning of one of the British campaigns in the French-Indian wars. Braddock later went on to disaster and death at Fort Duquesne.

When the capital city was under construction the nearest source of rock was the outcropping. It was blasted and cut for stone for government and private buildings and to line the C&O Canal until the outcropping was finally reduced to the size of a boulder, and the marshland was filled in.

Braddock's Rock, now a tiny remnant, deserves its place in history even if it is at the bottom of a well.

Pennsylvania Avenue and the Mall

Pennsylvania Avenue is the "famous mile" of the capital that stretches in a wide, unbroken vista from the White House to the Capitol. It is along this avenue that presidents parade to and from their inaugurations; that heroes are welcomed home from their achievements or travails; and that demonstrations surge in protest or support of an issue.

Just to the south of the avenue stretches the long carpet of green grass and trees and museums that make up the Mall.

These two areas contain many of the great cultural and historical treasures of the nation.

☞ *Archives*

The National Archives is one of the nation's most varied treasure troves. Enshrined here are priceless documents such as the Declaration of Independence and the Constitution of the United States, along with billions of other pieces of paper that record our history. The Archives is also the repository of some very strange objects.

For example, there are the personal photo album of Hitler's mistress Eva Braun; the unspeakable lampshade made of human skin from one of the victims of a Nazi concentration camp; the artifacts of the assassination of President John F. Kennedy, including the entire trauma room in the Dallas hospital where he was pronounced dead; and a small brown paper bag containing a hamburger with one bite missing.

The hamburger story happened in early 1940 when the U.S. Navy ship *Dubuque* was tied up at dock in Detroit. One of three or four girls who came aboard on a tour caught the eye of a sailor and struck up an acquaintanceship. She went ashore and brought back two hamburgers and sodas. The sailor and the girl found privacy in a gun locker aboard ship. She had been sniffing chloroform to get high and wasn't feeling well. She took one bite from the hamburger, vomited and shortly thereafter died. The sailor was charged with involuntary manslaughter and rape, and the hamburger was part of the evidence used in the trial. The sailor was acquitted, but the Archives got the hamburger.

There is another oddity in the collection at the Archives—an olive jar containing two severed little fingers. In 1918 Mexican bandits kidnapped two Americans, Otto Land and Gustavus Whiteford. To prove that they meant business, the bandits cut a little finger off each prisoner and sent the fingers in the olive jar along with their ransom demands. When the ransom was paid, Land was released but Whiteford was killed. The fingers were turned over to the State Department, which sent them to the Archives.

When something is sent to the Archives for safekeeping it will be kept safely—perhaps forever.

☞ *Temperance Fountain*

One of the more unusual landmarks on historic Pennsylvania Avenue is the Temperance Fountain at 7th Street. It is a sort of open temple with entwined dolphins on a pedestal in the center. On top of the structure is a water crane meant to symbolize the superior qualities of water over alcoholic beverages. At one time the dolphins provided refreshing iced water to weary tourists at this halfway point between the Capitol and the White House. But some years ago the city government stopped providing ice, and later the water was turned off.

This fountain and others like it were donated to Washington and other cities across the nation by Dr. Henry Cogswell of San Francisco. He was the first dentist in that California city and made his fortune in real estate and mining stocks. His great passions were temperance and the perpetuation of his name, hence the gifts of fountains.

It is reported that these unusual and awkward structures spurred the movement across the country for city fine arts commissions to screen such gifts. Washington's Temperance Fountain has prompted other reactions also. A passerby one day hung a wire coat hanger around the crane's neck where it stayed for years until it rusted away, and about 100 feet away from the fountain is one of the larger and better known liquor stores in Washington.

And, to keep alive the name of the good doctor, the nation's capital is home for the Cogswell Society, a convivial group of successful doctors, lawyers, journalists and other professionals who meet for luncheon each month. The chairman of the group is called the "lead Heron" and he ceremoniously opens each luncheon session by standing on one leg and offering this toast: "To temperance." The shouted reply from members and guests, also standing on one leg, is "I'll drink to that."

☞ *Hookers*

Have you ever wondered how prostitutes came to be called hookers? They were named after a general in the U.S. Army.

Before the outbreak of the Civil War, Washington was a rather sleepy, quiet southern town. But by the fall of 1863, the population had doubled, and, according to local police officials, prostitutes, gamblers, thieves and the worst of the riff-raff of other cities had gathered in the capital where the money was easy and the tiny police force was all but helpless. There was certainly a problem; the *Washington Star* denied reports that there were 15,000 prostitutes in the capital, based on its own tally which turned up a mere 3,900 practitioners of the ancient profession.

The city council considered licensing houses of ill-fame, but before they could act, General Joseph Hooker rounded up the ladies of the evening and concentrated them in the triangle below Pennsylvania Avenue near the Treasury Department. There, in one area, surveillance was simple.

That section of Washington immediately became known as Joe Hooker's division, and prostitutes became known as hookers.

☞ *Whistler*

The Freer Gallery on the Mall is frequently overlooked by visitors to Washington who probably don't know that it has, perhaps, the finest collection of oriental art in America. It also has the world's largest collection of the works of the great American artist James McNeil Whistler, including the portrait *Princess from the Land of Porcelain* and the stunning Peacock Room he designed especially to showcase that portrait.

A wealthy British shipowner, Frederick R. Leyland, owned the *Princess* portrait. To properly display it, he retained a designer to create a room for it in his London home.

When the room was completed Whistler was invited to view it. He was pleased with the place of honor for his portrait of the *Princess*, but objected to the surroundings. He persuaded Leyland to permit him to tone down the room.

Whistler started by painting out the red flowers on the wall and cutting off the red border of the rug. He then painted over the expensive and historic leather walls, adopting huge peacocks as a decorative motif.

Leyland was appalled by what Whistler had done and asked the artist what he owed him for wrecking his dining room. The artist promptly replied, "A thousand guineas." "No," said Leyland, "a thousand pounds," the coin of the tradesman rather than the artist. This slight infuriated Whistler, but he finished the room by painting two more peacocks on the wall opposite the *Princess* portrait. They are caricatures of himself and Leyland. One peacock is clutching a mass of silver shillings, its body smothered in gold coins. The other is prancing triumphantly in disdain, the air filled with flying feathers.

Years later Charles L. Freer, founder of the Freer Gallery of Art, purchased the Peacock Room and made it part of the museum on the Mall.

Whistler is best known for one painting, *Whistler's Mother.* The Freer Gallery has the companion painting that few people know exists—*Whistler's Father.*

☞ *National Theatre*

Legend has it that an actor is buried under the stage at the National Theatre and that his ghost has been seen wandering around from time to time.

The National, which has been at the same location on E Street between 14th and 13th Streets since 1835, is one of the oldest and most historic theaters in America.

In the 19th century actors were not paid very much, and, because the profession was looked down upon, they frequently used stage names rather than their own, making their true identities difficult to trace.

One day at the National, two actors were down in the basement washing their clothes. They got into an argument, probably over an ingenue. One killed the other and promptly buried him in an area between the theater's old and new foundation walls. The area is now known as the cemetery.

In about 1896 an employee of the theater who knew the dead actor by his stage name, John McCollough, recognized him walking around the stage and called to him, but he vanished. McCollough has been seen a number of times since. His real name has never been known. Four or five years ago electricians digging in the basement uncovered a metal object that Smithsonian technicians identified as a piece of a Springfield military musket. It could be part of the murder weapon.

There are a number of other stories about the old theater. One is that President Lincoln and his guests had reservations to attend a performance at the National on the night of April 14, 1865, but they decided to go to Ford's Theatre instead. John Wilkes Boothe, who had access to the National because he was an actor, was sitting in the mezzanine foyer writing letters when he learned of the change in the President's plans. He left at once to prepare for that night at Ford's Theatre.

☞ *Petersen House*

One of the few places in the nation where the overwhelming tragedy and impact of an event in history becomes clear and painfully real is the small bedroom in the Petersen House across the street from Ford's Theatre. This is where President Abraham Lincoln died.

The room is furnished as it was the night the dying Lincoln lay unconscious while the great of the nation paid a last visit. Oddly, the room is approximately the same size as the tiny log cabin where the President was born.

Even more ironic is the fact that a few weeks before he assassinated the President, actor John Wilkes Booth had rented the same room in the Petersen House and had slept in the very bed where his victim later died.

One other coincidence is associated with that event. Behind Ford's Theatre is a now bricked-in archway over an alley that was used by a funeral home in business at the time. Four years after his death in a barn on a Virginia farm, the government gave the body of John Wilkes Booth to his family. The family arranged, by sheer coincidence, with the funeral home behind Ford's Theatre to have the body shipped to Baltimore, where it is now interred. Thus, Booth left Washington for the last time from the same alley he used to escape Ford's Theatre after assassinating Lincoln.

☞ *Smithson's Will*

The Smithsonian Institution is one of the world's greatest centers of research and learning, and its collection of museums and galleries is without peer. But it might never have existed.

James Smithson was an Englishman who had not visited the United States. Nevertheless, he left his entire fortune of about $500,000 to the United States to establish an institution for the "diffusion of knowledge."

No one really knows why he left his money to this nation rather than to his homeland or to one of its institutions. However, the story generally accepted is this. Smithson was the illegitimate son of the first Duke of Northumberland. He felt keenly the ostracism and lack of acceptance by society. Perhaps Smithson felt that the United States, with its less structured social system and emphasis on freedom and liberty, was more worthy to carry out his lofty purpose.

Smithson, who wrote his will in 1826 and died in 1829, left his fortune to his nephew, provided that the nephew had children. The United States had to wait until 1835 when the nephew died childless to claim the bequest. Had the nephew fathered heirs, there would have been no Smithsonian Institution.

There was another complication, however: it took the Congress 11 years of debate to determine what to do with the money. Some members of Congress opposed accepting that or any other bequest from a private person.

The gift was finally accepted in 1846, and the Congress established the Smithsonian Institution.

☞ Oldest Elevator

One of America's major contributions to architecture is the skyscraper. That advance in building construction was made possible by the invention of the safety elevator by Elisha Graves Otis.

In 1852 Otis was working for a bedstead manufacturing company in Yonkers, New York. Because the hoist used to lift heavy machinery fell from time to time with disastrous results, the inventor set about devising a machine that could be relied upon. He hit upon the idea of using a good, tough, steel wagon spring that meshed with a ratchet on two sides of the elevator shaft. If the rope broke the spring would catch and hold. Otis didn't know that his simple device would alter the face of the world.

The Crystal Palace Exposition was held in New York in 1854. It was the perfect theater for demonstrating the safety device.

With a large audience on hand, drawn by the danger of the drama, Otis ascended in an elevator cradled in an open-sided shaft. Halfway up he had the hoisting rope cut with an axe. The safety device held, the elevator did not fall, Otis was not injured and the skyscraper was on its way.

In 1826 a four-story building was erected at 637 Indiana Avenue, N.W., to house a grocery store. The area, known as Market Square, was a forerunner of today's shopping mall. Within a year after Otis demonstrated his elevator at the Crystal Palace in 1854 an identical elevator was installed in the Indiana Avenue building. It is still there and still operates very nicely.

The building is now occupied by Litwin Furniture, and the owner uses the ancient device to haul his goods from floor to floor. The motive power is supplied by a rope and counterweights. The elevator hasn't needed major repair work in more than 130 years. It passes elevator inspection every six months.

Litwin may have the oldest operating elevator in the nation.

Statues and Plaques

Scattered all over the Washington area are statues, plaques and markers relating to persons or events that once were of utmost significance, but over the years have faded from memory or importance.

Sometimes these memorials tell a poignant or humorous story or stand in disapproval of forgetfulness.

☞ *Equestrian Statues*

Legends in Washington have a life of their own—they refuse to die. One of the most persistent alleges that one can tell how many times the person honored by a statue was wounded in war by the number of legs the horse he is riding has lifted off the pedestal.

Not true. For example:

• The horse carrying Lt. General George Washington in Washington Circle has one leg off the ground, but the first President was never wounded.

● The horse carrying General William T. Sherman in the statue near the White House has all four hooves firmly planted, although Sherman was wounded in the Battle of Shiloh, also called Pittsburg Landing.

● And, if the legend were true, the statue of General James B. McPherson in McPherson Square should be lying down. The General was killed in the Battle of Atlanta.

☞ *General Scott*

There is a horse in Washington that underwent a sex-change operation. It was painless and was performed without anaesthesia because the horse is bronze. He, originally, she, is the proud steed of Lt. General Winfield Scott.

The equestrian statue stands in the center of Scott Circle and portrays General Scott peering with fixed eyes at the White House just six blocks away down 16th Street. (He longed to occupy the executive mansion but, as the Whig candidate for president in 1852, was roundly defeated by Franklin Pierce.)

Scott, known as "old Fuss and Feathers," served the country in the military for more than 50 years and was the commanding officer of the United States Army longer than any man in history. The high point of his career was his triumph in the war with Mexico. The bronze for the statue came from melted down cannon captured by Scott's command in that conflict.

In his later years, at the outbreak of the Civil War, the General was old, obese and racked with pain from arthritis and other ailments. His physical condition forced him to ride a quiet, comfortable mare.

The sculptor commissioned to create the memorial to General Scott, Henry Kirke Brown, knew that Scott rode a mare. When the model was completed and before the bronze casting began (unlike the Truman version of the story), some of Scott's descendants saw the artist's work and protested vehemently because no general was ever depicted for history riding a small, placid mare.

After much heated argument the sculptor made the necessary adjustments, calling his handiwork a "reduced stallion." And so Lt. General Winfield Scott, military hero and presidential candidate, sits on an altered mare.

☞ *Other Statues*

There are other odd stories about statues in Washington. The one about Lafayette in the square across from the White House is best appreciated if told in the middle of a Washington winter when there is snow on the ground and the wind is sweeping across the large, open square.

Lafayette, in civilian clothes, is portrayed seeking aid from his native France for the colonists' war of independence. A huge heavy cloak swirls on his left arm, and at his feet is a representation of America. Her lovely figure is nude from the waist up and she holds in her right hand the sword of valor. In cold and snowy weather she seems to be saying, "General, here is your sword, but for God's sake give me that cloak."

On Scott Circle Dr. Samuel Hahnemann sits brooding in the center of an impressive curved bench. In Leipzig, Germany, in 1879, he discovered and practiced homeopathic medicine, which reached its height of acceptance in the United States in the early part of the 20th century.

● The *Titanic* Memorial along the Washington channel waterfront at 4th and P Streets, S.W., honors the men aboard that doomed vessel who gave their lives so that women and children aboard ship could be saved. The money for the memorial was raised from among the survivors. The sculptor was a woman, Gertrude Vanderbilt Whitney.

Mrs. Whitney, the daughter of the fabled Cornelius Vanderbilt, was a socially prominent and very wealthy woman. A talented sculptress in her own right, she created the Whitney Studio Club in New York to encourage other American artists. This group formed the basis for the Whitney Museum of American Art, which she founded.

Mrs. Whitney also was the principal figure in the famous New York court battle for the custody of her niece Gloria Vanderbilt.

By a quirk of fate, shortly after Mrs. Whitney had completed a model for the statue of the *Titanic* she lost her own brother, Alfred Gwynne Vanderbilt, when the *Lusitania* was sunk by a German submarine on May 7, 1915.

● Along the riverfront near the Lincoln Memorial is a monument honoring John Ericsson. He was an inventor and designer who perfected the screw propellor, thus revolutionizing navigation. Ericsson designed the ironclad union ship, the *Monitor*, that was engaged in the famous Civil War naval battle with the *Merrimac* in 1862 and changed naval warfare for all time.

• Ward Circle at Massachusetts and Nebraska Avenues, N.W., is graced by a tall statue of Major General Arte*mas* Ward. He is not to be confused with the 19th-century dialect humorist, Arte*mus* Ward. The Ward in the circle was the first commander of the "patriotic" forces in the Revolutionary War. He was in charge of the siege of Boston, then held by British troops, until he was relieved by General George Washington. Ward was a distinguished alumnus of Harvard University, which provided the funds for the statue. It was supposed to be equestrian but the high cost of bronze just before the outbreak of World War II eliminated the horse, which is why Major General Ward stands on his own two feet at the busy intersection.

• One of the most ambiguous statues in Washington is in the front yard of a house at 601 North Carolina Avenue, S.E. The rather lonely, wistful figure is that of Olive Risley Seward, the daughter of Lincoln's secretary of state, William H. Seward. The sculptor wanted to memorialize a member of Secretary Seward's family and chose Seward's foster daughter Olive as the subject. Why she was chosen or why the sculpture was placed in this most unusual location is not clear, except that Olive seems to be looking toward Seward Square just a few feet from the front yard of the house.

☞ *Albert Pike*

There is a little known secret about the life of Albert Pike, whose statue stands in an out-of-the-way location at 3rd and D Streets, N.W. He seems rather lonely there, off the mainstream of monumental Washington. The District police at their headquarters next door and the scurrying clerks from the Labor Department to the east pay little attention to the statue of the sturdy figure who gazes steadfastly—and significantly—to the north.

Pike had a varied career as a poet, newspaper publisher, western adventurer and, finally, as one of the highest ranking officials of the Masonic order. He served as the sovereign grand commander of the Scottish Rite of Freemasonry from 1859 to 1891, and it was this office that earned him his place of honor in a city of memorials.

The secret is that, despite the civilian clothes, the long flowing hair and the book of Masonry in his hand, Albert Pike was a general in the Confederate Army. He is the only rebel military officer honored with an outdoor statue in Washington, and for many years was remembered in annual services held at the statue by the United Daughters of the Confederacy.

☞ *Walter Reed Fountain*

Sometimes an artist commissioned to produce a work lets his imagination run wild. And sometimes he is given fanciful or inaccurate information that adversely affects his work. Something of the sort happened in the planning and execution of the "penguin" fountain in front of the central building of the Walter Reed Army Medical Center on upper 16th Street, N.W.

The memorial fountain, which honors Colonel John Van Rensselaer Hoff, was made possible by a gift from his widow.

There is no question that Colonel Hoff was a distinguished army medical officer: his major accomplishment after his retirement and recall to active duty in World War I was reorganization of the Medical Corps, which up to that time had had little or no recognition. Hoff insisted upon and won the battle to give corps personnel all the rights and privileges of regular army officers. He also greatly improved the efficiency and effectiveness of the Medical Corps.

In designing the fountain the architect took into account Hoff's service in the tropics, the Philippines and in the Arctic as an observer with the Russian army. Hence, the fountain's penguins, which spout water from their mouths, and their pedestals, on which cobras have been carved.

The trouble is there are no penguins in the Arctic, only in the Antarctic.

☞ *Plaques*

One of the more rewarding pastimes in Washington is finding and reading plaques. They are all over town and commemorate events, historical moments and important sites or structures that once occupied space but were destroyed.

● Sung Song Lung, a Chinese grocery store and carry-out, occupies the ground floor of a small building with a sinister history at 604 H Street, N.W. This building was the boarding house, operated by Mrs. Mary Surratt, where the conspirators met to plot the assassination of President Abraham Lincoln. A plaque commemorates that segment of history. It was not put there by a federal agency, a private foundation or even a prestigious historical society, but by the Chi-Am Lion's Club of Washington. The Club wanted to call attention to the historic building standing in the middle of Chinatown. The plaque says: A Historical Landmark/Surratt Boarding House/Conspirators plotted the abduction of U.S. President Abraham Lincoln/Plaque by Chi-Am Lion's Club.

● The late New York financier Bernard Baruch, who was called upon for advice by many presidents of the United States, often sat on a particular bench in Lafayette Square across the street from the White House. From his bench he could gaze in contemplation at the executive mansion or chat with friends about high government policy. Today, standing by that bench is a marker commemorating it as the "Bernard Baruch Bench of Inspiration." The marker was put there by the Boy Scouts of America.

● On the grounds of the Columbia Hospital for Women just off Pennsylvania Avenue at 25th Street, N.W., is an obscure marker commemorating a most significant event—the signing of the Rush-Bagot Treaty. Except for historians, diplomats and a few other specialists, most people have never heard of the treaty, but its signing was a most significant event in North American history.

The Treaty of Ghent that ended the War of 1812 with Britain set up a number of commissions to settle various disputes. In 1817 acting U.S. Secretary of State Richard Rush met with British Minister Sir Charles Bagot in a mansion that then occupied the hospital grounds and has since been razed. They signed what has become known as the Rush-Bagot Treaty, ending warfare on the Great Lakes and thus demilitarizing the entire border between the United States and Canada. It remains the longest open and undefended border between two sovereign nations in the world.

● On the wall of the Pennsylvania Avenue side of the Willard Hotel is a plaque about Julia Ward Howe. Late in 1861 Mrs. Howe, along with President Lincoln and other high government officials, attended a massive military review of Union forces in nearby Virginia. She was so impressed with the spectacle that she came right back to her Willard Hotel room and wrote *The Battle Hymn of the Republic*.

● One of the most poignant plaques in Washington is practically unknown. It is built into the front wall of the old Vigilante Firehouse on Wisconsin Avenue a few feet away from the C&O Canal. The plaque reads simply: Bush, the old firedog/died of poison/July 5th, 1869/R.I.P.

Washington National Cathedral

The dominant structure on the northwest Washington skyline is the National Cathedral, officially known as the Cathedral Church of Saint Peter and Saint Paul. It sits in all its 14th-century Gothic splendor on the highest point in the city, Mount St. Albans. The cathedral was begun in 1907 and, when finished, will be one of the largest churches in the world.

Although Protestant Episcopal, the church is truly a National Cathedral because it has served as a spiritual gathering place for any number of other faiths including a congregation of Jewish worshipers and Muslim groups.

The National Cathedral is also, to a limited degree, an American Westminster Abbey. Interred in a marble sarcophagus is the body of President Woodrow Wilson. The crusaders sword carved on Wilson's tomb recalls his valiant battle for peace. Admiral George Dewey of Spanish-American-War fame is also interred in the cathedral. So are Helen Keller and her teacher-companion Anne Sullivan Macy; Mabel Boardman, long time head of the American Red Cross; and Cordell Hull, secretary of state during World War II.

☞ *Cathedral Art*

The massive beauty of the Washington National Cathedral is truly awe inspiring, but there are enough historic sidelights to give it a human dimension as well.

On the Churchill Porch inside the southwest corner of the cathedral, for example, is an iron gate given to honor the memory of Alvin McCauley, the founder of the Packard Motor Car company, which produced one of the luxury cars of its day. Woven into the design of the gate is the distinctive hub cap and radiator of the once famous Packard automobile.

On the end of an arm of a choir stall near the high altar is a tiny wood carving about the size of an American silver dollar. The imaginative and prophetic carver, who made the small medallion before the end of World War II, depicted the British lion crushing a serpent. The head of the serpent is the face of Adolph Hitler.

Outside, on the cathedral walls and towers, imagination and skill have run wild in a carefully planned way. To properly appreciate the gargoyles, grotesques and angels that add so much to the building, binoculars are helpful. Angels are part of the message of the cathedral. Most are placed high on the towers from where they can look down on the more mundane and less spiritual carvings. The gargoyles and grotesques do more than just add flavor to the building; they drain excess rain water away from the walls to prevent deterioration and staining.

In many cases the stone carver was given a free hand to sculpt the gargoyles and grotesques as he wished within the bounds of good taste and the religious theme of the cathedral. The result is what may be the largest assemblage of fanciful sculpture in the country.

● One patron of the cathedral who wished to commemorate her two adorable and mischievous grandsons, donated two gargoyles, one of a youngster with his hand in a cookie jar and the other, with a broken wagon by his side. Each has a broken halo around his head.

● The former headmistress of the National Cathedral School for Girls, Miss Catherine Lee, had a dog who regularly attacked the groundskeepers. The grotesque dedicated to her depicts a dog with a piece of a groundskeeper's pants in its mouth.

● A dog also plays a part in the sculpture for Canon Charles Martin, former headmaster of St. Albans School for Boys. The Canon's dog is a very ugly and fat English Bulldog.

● One of the loveliest events at the cathedral is the Christmas morning service, which has been broadcast on NBC television for more than 25 years. To honor the original producer of the television program, Doris Ann, is a grotesque depicting yards of scattered video tape and a TV camera turret. The grotesque honoring the first director of the program, Dick Cox, has the head of a rooster.

● One grotesque depicts a dentist working on a giant molar. Another shows a golfer's hands on a club as a reminder of a donor's absorbing hobby, and still another shows the cathedral's master carver blowing his top—his hat is being lifted into the air.

There are owls, lions, dragons, horses, cats, fish, a rhinoceros, an elephant, a ram, and a gargoyle that the carver was directed to make as ugly as possible. And he succeeded—beautifully.

☞ George Washington Statue

On the grounds of the Washington National Cathedral, below the south transcept at the bottom of the Pilgrim Steps, is one of the most interesting statues of the Father of our Country. The bronze Washington appears as if he had just ridden out of the woods and discovered Mount St. Albans to be the ideal place for a magnificent church. Indeed, it is likely that Washington *did* ride through the area in looking over the land for the future nation's capital.

The statue is notable in that the face of Washington is taken from a Rembrandt Peale painting owned by the cathedral, and the horse's eyes are of glass in the Egyptian style. But it is the horse that is more remarkable.

Shortly before the sculptor, Herbert Hazeltine, made the equestrian statue of George Washington at the cathedral, he executed a statue of the great race horse Man-o-War, which stands today in the Kentucky Horse Park in Lexington.

The two horses are almost identical—sculptor Hazeltine put George Washington on Man-o-War. One critic of the statue said after it was unveiled in 1957, "George looks like Willie Hartack," the famous jockey.

Georgetown

Georgetown has often been referred to as a "state of mind" as well as a location. It began as a seaport, a trading center, a residential area; became a neighborhood for low income workers and blacks; and was revived as a prestigious, chic area with high-cost homes and expensive shops and restaurants.

Today Georgetown has a warm, neighborhood feeling replete with history and charm.

☞ *Georgetown University*

The first non-Indian visitor to Georgetown was the legendary Captain John Smith who sailed up the Potomac as far as the Little Falls in 1608. He thought the place was delightful. Georgetown has been that way ever since, except for a few years here and there.

By the middle of the 18th century, Georgetown was a small collection of homes, taverns and warehouses that owed their existence to the great Maryland and Virginia commodity, tobacco.

The original survey in 1752 plotted a city of 60 acres from what is now 30th Street to Georgetown University and from N Street to the river. The two men from whose farmland the city was established grumbled mightily but accepted in compensation 280 pounds and two city lots. There were only 80 lots in the whole town.

From that meager beginning sprang a bustling community and a prestigious university.

John Carroll, the first Roman Catholic Bishop in America, founded the Georgetown Academy in 1789. From that grew the Georgetown University of today. At the entrance to the campus, a bronze likeness of Bishop Carroll sits in serene guardianship over the young men and women of Georgetown University. On almost any campus in the nation statues like this are fair game for student pranks. In this case the sculptor asked for them by leaving an open space under the Bishop's chair. Almost from the time the statue was placed on the campus, chamberpots have appeared and re-appeared in that inviting location. There was no way such a prank could be stopped by the good Jesuit fathers of the university, so in keeping with their renowned ability to cope, they filled the vacant space under the chair with books of unmovable bronze.

Just behind the statue of Bishop Carroll and in front of the massive Healy building are two ancient and worn cannon. They were brought to this country on the *Ark* and the *Dove*, the two tiny ships that carried the first Catholic settlers to the new world in 1633. The next year the settlers founded the colony of Maryland.

The cannon were a sidelight in the bitter political campaign of 1928 when Al

Smith, the Democratic candidate, became the first Catholic to run for president. Though it has never been confirmed, flamboyant Senator Tom Heflin of Alabama is reported to have charged that the two cannon on the grounds of Georgetown University were pointed directly at the Capitol building of the United States and could be used to intimidate Congress if Al Smith was elected president. Actually, the guns are aimed more to the soaring dome of the Shrine of the Immaculate Conception.

One of the most notable persons identified with Georgetown University was its 29th president, the Jesuit Father Patrick F. Healy. He assumed the office of acting president in 1873 and because of his work, dedication and ability became known as the second founder of Georgetown. Born in Georgia, he graduated from Holy Cross College in Massachusetts and received his post graduate education in Europe. At Georgetown Father Healy upgraded the curriculum and reorganized both the medical and law schools. Uppermost in his mind was the construction of a new building to provide more classrooms and living space for the students. The Healy building, landmark of Georgetown University with its massive tower, was completed in 1879.

Father Patrick F. Healy was black. Under the law of Georgia he was born a slave, although his father was an Irishman who had immigrated to this country and married a former slave. Father Healy was the first black to hold a Ph.D. in America and the first black president of a major, predominantly white university.

Georgetown University athletic teams are called "Hoyas." It is not known with absolute certainty where that name came from. The generally accepted story is that one day, years ago, a Georgetown team was playing a particularly brilliant defensive game and the partisans in the stands, to honor and encourage their team, began a chant or a cheer. Now, for such a prestigious academic institution plain, simple English just wouldn't do, and from the stands came the roar of "Oi," which translated from the Greek means the exclamation "Oh." The second word of the chant was "Saxa," which translated from the Latin means "rocks." So, loosely translated, "Oi saxa" means "Oh those rocks." Over the years the phrase was shortened to the present day "Hoya."

Far from the athletic fields, tucked away in a secure vault, is one of Georgetown's most precious possessions: the handwritten original manuscript of Mark Twain's *Tom Sawyer.* Mrs. Nicholas Brady of New York gave the manuscript to the University.

Mrs. Brady's late husband had amassed a distinguished collection of books and manuscripts in American and English literature. The centerpiece of his collection was the Tom Sawyer manuscript, which he had acquired when in 1873 he purchased the estate of Walter Bliss, the son of Twain's American publisher, Elisha Bliss.

Mrs. Brady presented the manuscript to Georgetown University and was later awarded an honorary Doctor of Law degree for her outstanding promotion of Jesuit education. She was the first woman to receive a degree from the then all-male university.

☞ Gun Barrel Fence

Any number of historic and memorable houses still stand in Georgetown. Volumes have been written about them, both individually and collectively. One short row is especially intriguing.

A man named Reuben Daw owned a large part of a block bounded by 28th and 29th Streets and P and Q Streets. In 1848–49 he built a number of houses along the north side of P Street in the 2800 block. This was shortly after the end of the war with Mexico. Daw needed an additional touch for his newly built homes, and the War Department had for sale a large quantity of muskets that had been condemned as junk. Daw bought them and lined them up to form a fence in front of his houses.

If you look closely you can still see the aiming sights on the ends of the gun barrels.

☞ Henry Foxall

Henry Foxall was born in England in 1758, the son of an obscure blacksmith. He learned the skills of the iron founder in the "works" near Birmingham and in 1797 came to the colonies and established a foundry in Philadelphia. When the capital of the new nation was built along the Potomac, Foxall, at Thomas

Jefferson's urging, built a new foundry on the river in Georgetown.

The government was interested in Foxall because he forged the best cannon in the nation; he produced many of them for both the army and the navy.

It is important to point out also that Foxall was a devout Methodist, a lay preacher and a big contributor to the church in Washington.

In 1814 the war with Great Britain moved into the nation's capital with a vengeance when the British sailed up the Potomac, landed in Maryland, captured the city and burned the Capitol and the White House. One prize they wanted to destroy was Foxall's foundry in Georgetown, a major source of American armaments.

Foxall knew this, and devout man that he was, he prayed, vowing that if his foundry was spared he would make a "thanks" offering to God.

Before the British could move onto Georgetown from Washington on that sultry August day designated for the attack, a violent summer thunderstorm swept Washington, making troop movements impossible. The next day the British evacuated Washington. Foxall's foundry had been spared.

True to his word, Henry Foxall began building a new Methodist Church at 14th and G Streets, N.W. It was dedicated in September 1815 and was named Foundry Methodist Church. It is now located on 16th Street, N.W., and may be the only religious center in the nation named for a munitions plant.

No one really knows why, over the years, an additional letter *h* has been added to the Henry Foxall name. Today, Washingtonians are reminded of the religious munitions maker by Foxhall Road, which cuts through one of the more affluent neighborhoods in Washington.

☞ *C&O Canal*

As the new United States of America developed as a nation it became apparent that the commercial areas of the east coast had to be joined to the productive territories of the west. Better and cheaper transportation of goods and raw materials was needed. Waterways were ideal—and that meant canals had to be built.

George Washington tried to build a canal around the falls of the Potomac, but failed. Later he and others conceived the C&O Canal to link the Potomac waterway with the rich Shenandoah and Ohio river valleys, a project that was absolutely necessary to the survival of Georgetown and Alexandria as ports.

Construction on the C&O Canal began on July 4, 1828, with President John Quincy Adams turning the first shovel of earth. In Georgetown on Wisconsin Avenue next to the canal and a few blocks from where tourists board the canal barge is a nondescript obelisk, almost hidden by trees and brush, commemorating this event that promised such a golden future.

On that same day in 1828, Charles Carroll "of Carrollton," a signer of the Declaration of Independence, turned the first shovel of dirt in Baltimore to begin the construction of the Baltimore and Ohio Railroad.

Although it was not recognized at the moment and it would not be apparent for years, on that first day the canals lost the race with the railroads to unite the east coast with the west.

☞ *Suter's Tavern*

One of the most historic buildings in Washington has disappeared. No one knows with absolute certainty where in Georgetown Suter's Tavern, also called the Fountain Inn, was located.

As a bustling seaport and trade center, Georgetown needed a number of inns to accommodate itinerant travelers and merchants. Among the most famous was the Fountain Inn, operated by John Suter. It was there that George Washington met in late March of 1791 with the three major landowners from whose holdings the new federal city was to be created. Had the negotiations not been successful the capital might have been located elsewhere.

Later, Major Pierre L'Enfant and Andrew Ellicott used Suter's Tavern as their headquarters while they surveyed and planned the federal city.

In September of 1791 Thomas Jefferson and James Madison met there with the three commissioners selected by Washington to govern the capital to be.

The presidential election of 1800 was thrown into the House of Representatives, whose members met and decided—at Suter's Tavern—that Thomas Jefferson would prevail over John Adams. The report at the time was that the election was "very wet."

Eventually John Suter moved to the Union Tavern in Georgetown; the old Fountain Inn went through a number of proprietorships and finally disappeared. But the dispute over the location of Suter's Tavern continues. In 1953 Cornelius Heine, then a National Park Service historian, conducted an exhaustive study and concluded the tavern was located on the northwest corner of 31st Street and what is now K Street, and a plaque was placed there.

Later, research by Oliver W. Holmes, a leading local historian, placed Suter's Tavern on the east side of Wisconsin Avenue just north of the bridge over the C&O Canal. There is no plaque there.

Nearby Washington

Washington, D.C. is an artificial enclave carved out of Maryland and Virginia. People lived and events occurred outside the enclave both before and after it was created.

Maryland's contribution to the ten-mile square federal city was land taken from Montgomery County and included the then major port-city of Georgetown and several other smaller settlements.

Virginia contributed land from Fairfax County and the other port-city of Alexandria. The two halves of the federal enclave were split by the Potomac River.

The residents of both cities and of the rural farmland that made up the District of Columbia did not like the idea of becoming part of an unknown jurisdiction.

Georgetown wanted to remain in Maryland, and Alexandria, as a matter of pride and history, bitterly resisted leaving Virginia.

In the early part of the 19th century, as the clamor against slavery became louder and louder, the slave owners and traders of Alexandria and the Virginia portion of the District became more and more apprehensive that slavery would be abolished and they would lose valuable property and a way of life. They found the issue of no federal presence in the area and began the movement to return what is now Arlington County to the state of Virginia.

In 1846 the campaign bore fruit. The Congress retroceded the area to Virginia. The formal excuse for this transfer was in one of the "whereas" clauses of the resolution. It said in part that there "has not been, nor is there likely to be" a use of the land by the federal government; therefore, it should be retroceded to Virginia.

Of course no one could foresee the Pentagon, the Navy Annex, National Airport, or Fort Myer and all of the other appendages of the federal government that have spilled across the Potomac from the District.

IN VIRGINIA

☞ *Fort Myer*

There is a horse buried on the hallowed parade grounds of Fort Myer, the prestigious army post just across the Potomac in Virginia.

Not a triple crown winner, nor even a thoroughbred, he is best remembered as the riderless horse that led the funeral procession of President John F. Kennedy. His name was Blackjack after the commander of U.S. forces in World War I and General of the Armies John J. Pershing.

Blackjack was the last quartermaster horse issued by the army, and the last to be branded U.S.A. He served not only in the funeral of Kennedy, but also for Presidents Herbert Hoover and Lyndon Johnson, and for General Douglas MacArthur.

When death came to Blackjack on February 6, 1976, he was buried on the parade grounds with special military honors. His admirers erected a small memorial to him.

It was from this same parade ground at Fort Myer that the first military test flight of an airplane took place on October 3, 1908. Orville Wright succeeded in keeping his fragile aircraft aloft for one minute and eleven seconds. On the second test flight two weeks later army Lt. Thomas Selfridge accompanied Wright. The plane had been airborne for four minutes when a propeller broke and the aircraft went out of control. Wright was injured in the crash, but Selfridge died. He was the first military air casualty of the age of flight.

☞ *Bailey's Crossroads*

Bailey's Crossroads is a major shopping and residential area in Virginia just a few minutes' drive from the nation's capital. Originally, it was part of George Washington's northern tract holdings.

In December of 1837 Hachaliah Bailey bought about 500 acres at the intersection, but he did not buy the land just for farming. A businessman from New

York, Bailey was deeply involved in circuses. He also bought the land because he needed winter quarters for his circus.

Bailey built his home, called Maury, at the crossroads along with barns and sheds and a riding ring to train circus acts. Great excitement enveloped the rural Virginia area when the small collection of animals and performers gathered for their annual winter sojourn at Bailey's Crossroads.

Years later the Bailey circus was combined with that of P. T. Barnum's, and the result was Barnum and Bailey's Greatest Show on Earth.

☞ *Dinosaur Tracks*

Dinosaurs—fairly big ones—roamed around the Washington area 200 million years ago. The huge beasts were common in the western United States, but on the east coast tracings of them have been found only in this area and in the Connecticut River valley.

The story of the discovery of dinosaurs in the Washington area is remarkable in itself.

When James Monroe was president of the United States in 1820 he built his home, called Oak Hill, just south of Leesburg, Virginia. His friend Thomas Jefferson and architect James Hoban helped design it. It was at Oak Hill that the President wrote his famous Monroe Doctrine.

In the early 1920s the then owner of the home decided to expand it in keeping with the original plans by adding gardens, walkways and outdoor terraces. Stonemasons used the outcropping of slate or shale on the property as the source of the flagstone slabs needed for the new construction. Rather odd markings on the slates were authenticated, on examination by experts, as dinosaur footprints, hide marks and tail draggings that were 200 million years old.

Oak Hill is a private residence and not open to the public, but occasionally tours of the grounds and the house are permitted. The tour includes the very rare sight of east coast dinosaur tracks.

IN MARYLAND

☞ *Cabin John Bridge*

In its early days Washington depended upon creeks, springs and public wells and pumps for its water supply. As the city grew, a new source of water in large volume had to be found.

In 1853 General Montgomery C. Meigs of the Army Corps of Engineers planned an aqueduct to bring water from the Great Falls of the Potomac to the city. To bring the water over the deep valley of Cabin John Run, he built a stone bridge. It was a marvel of engineering and, when finished, was the longest stone arch of its type in the world. It may still be.

When the aqueduct was authorized by Congress, Franklin Pierce was president and Jefferson Davis was secretary of war. When it was finished Abraham Lincoln was president. A large plaque was installed on the bridge abutment to commemorate the engineering achievement.

After the outbreak of the Civil War the Secretary of the Interior noticed the plaque and was horrified to see the name of Jefferson Davis, president of the Confederacy, on the same memorial as that of Abraham Lincoln. He ordered Davis's name chiseled away, and for years after the war there was a blank line on the plaque. Descendants of Jefferson Davis and other sympathetic groups protested this insult and lobbied vigorously to have the wrong corrected. Finally, President Theodore Roosevelt ordered a new plaque made to include the names of both Davis and Lincoln.

The plaque with both names is there today on the Cabin John Aqueduct Bridge. It is perhaps the only place in the nation where the names of the president of the United States and the president of the Confederacy appear together.

☞ *The First President's Grave*

The burial places where the earthly remains of our presidents lie in rest often become shrines, like the simple tomb of George Washington on the hillside at Mount Vernon; the more elaborate tomb of Abraham Lincoln in Springfield, Illinois; and John F. Kennedy's eternal flame burning in the quiet of Arlington

Cemetery. But the last resting place of the first president of the United States elected "in Congress assembled" is not known.

He was John Hanson of Maryland, an outstanding patriot leader.

Hanson was chairman of the Maryland delegation to the Continental Congress when the Articles of Confederation were approved in 1781. He was then elected president of the United States by the Congress under the terms of the document that had just been put into effect.

The Articles of Confederation were a disaster. Rather than creating a central government, the result was a kind of "union of friendship." The government had no power to tax and the levies were either ignored or paid only in part. The Congress could not regulate interstate commerce, and the result was a series of economic wars among the states. No central executive or judiciary authority that was effective existed.

John Hanson served a one-year term as president in 1781–82, and others followed him in that office. Among them were Richard Henry Lee of Virginia and John Hancock of Massachusetts. Hanson thus preceded George Washington, who was elected president under the terms of the new Constitution in 1789, by eight years.

In 1783 Hanson became ill and traveled to the home of his nephew in Oxon Hill, Maryland, now a suburb of Washington. There he died and, presumably, was buried on the estate. There is no marker, headstone or any other indication of where the body of the first president of the United States, John Hanson, lies buried.

☞ *Bladensburg Duelling Grounds*

What many know as Washington's "dark and bloody grounds" are just over the northeast District line in Prince George's County, Maryland. They are the Bladensburg duelling grounds where, until the middle of the 19th century, gentlemen settled their irreconcilable, and often trivial, differences with weapons. Over the years more than 50 duels were fought in the secluded glen.

Perhaps the most famous duel occurred in 1820 when former navy Commodore James Barron shot and killed Commodore Stephen Decatur, the naval hero of the Barbary pirate wars.

The most unusual and bloodiest duel, however, was fought the year before between Virginia Senator Armistead Mason and his brother-in-law John M. McCarty. It was over a dispute of less than earth shaking proportions, and McCarty, as the challenged party, had the choice of weapons.

He thought the whole idea ridiculous and suggested the two hold hands and jump from the dome of the Capitol building. Mason refused, and McCarty next proposed that the two of them sit on a keg of gunpowder and be blown up. That didn't sit well with the Senator, so the challenged party suggested daggers in a hand-to-hand fight. Mason rejected that also. Finally, McCarty selected shotguns at ten paces, which would be equivalent to sitting on the keg of gunpowder. Mason accepted. Before the duel, the agreement was modified to the use of muskets at 12 paces.

On the appointed day in 1819 the two men faced each other and, on the signal, fired simultaneously. Mason, who had issued the challenge, died at once. A Washington newspaper reported that the musket shot "put an immediate period to his existence."

McCarty was wounded in the arm and recovered, but the remainder of his life was filled with remorse. He was haunted by the affair at the "dark and bloody grounds" of Bladensburg.

☞ *Uncle Tom's Cabin*

President Abraham Lincoln once commented that the anti-slavery novel, *Uncle Tom's Cabin*, was the book that "made this big war." It was based on the life of a slave who lived and worked on a farm in Montgomery County, Maryland, just a few miles from the White House.

The slave, Josiah Henson, was born on a farm in Charles County, Maryland, and sold at age six to a tavern keeper in Rockville. Later he became the property of a farmer on Old Georgetown Road, who in 1825 sent Henson to work for his brother in Kentucky. The slave escaped five years later and fled to Canada. There Henson wrote three memoirs about his experiences as a slave. One of them, *The Life of Josiah Henson, Formerly a Slave*, was published in 1849. Harriet Beecher Stowe read it and then wrote *Uncle Tom's Cabin*.

The cabin of logs where Henson lived exists to this day as part of a house in

Montgomery County. It is a private home, and its owners do not want its exact location revealed. But Uncle Tom's cabin *is* there on Old Georgetown Road in Montgomery County.

Cemeteries

People's reactions to cemeteries vary widely. Some love them for the peace, quiet and serenity they offer, some look upon them as sculpture gardens and others think of them as great repositories of history. There are also, of course, those who would go miles out of their way to avoid passing by a cemetery.

The Washington area has an abundance of cemeteries, many of which contain the mortal remains of past movers and shakers of the earth or those whose lives provide colorful asides to history.

The following is about a few of those cemeteries.

☞ *Arlington National Cemetery*

Arlington National Cemetery is truly one of the nation's most hallowed shrines. Here rest the men and women who served in the nation's armed forces and in its government from the Revolution to the space age—its foot soldiers and its leaders, its plodders and its adventurers.

After General Robert E. Lee and his wife, who owned the property, left to join the Confederacy at the outbreak of the Civil War, the Union Army took over Arlington and its land as part of the defense of Washington. As casualties mounted and burial space became scarce, the Union decided to use the Lee property as a cemetery.

The quartermaster general of the union forces, Montgomery C. Meigs, directed that some of the first burials be made in the rose garden of the Lee mansion. Although Meigs was an Alabaman, he was deeply angered and hurt by what he regarded as the betrayal of the oath of loyalty Lee had taken as a U.S. Army officer. By burying union soldiers in close proximity to the mansion, Meigs felt he made it impossible for the Lees to return. They never did.

One of the more graphic and striking memorials in the cemetery marks the grave of Brevet Major John Rodgers Meigs, the son of the quartermaster general. The carving shows the young man as he was found dead on the battlefield near Harrisonburg, Virginia. Prone, in the uniform of a first lieutenant with his pistol on the ground at his side, young Meigs is hatless and the fatal wound is apparent.

The officer with the highest military rank ever conferred by the United States was General of the Armies John J. Pershing, commander of the Allied Expeditionary Forces in World War I. His is one of the simplest markers—the regular government-issue, white marble headstone. Many years before his death, General Pershing selected the marker and location of his grave. He said he wanted to be at rest near the brave comrades who served with him in World War I.

Unknown soldiers of every war the United States has ever fought except the Revolutionary War and the war with Mexico are honored in Arlington Cemetery. The tomb of the unknown soldier of the Revolutionary War is in the quiet churchyard of the Old Presbyterian Meeting House in Alexandria. There are dead of the war with Mexico in Arlington Cemetery, and one or more of them may be unknown.

Under one large memorial lie the bodies of 2,111 unknown union soldiers of the Civil War gathered from the battlefields near Washington. The unknown servicemen of World Wars I and II and the Korean conflict are entombed in the classic plaza overlooking the city of Washington. An empty crypt at the tomb site may someday hold an unknown of the Vietnam war, but at this time it remains empty. There are servicemen missing in action, but no unknowns. Many confederate unknown soldiers are buried in Arlington, most of them around the confederate memorial. The headstones of the confederate dead differ from those of others: they are slightly pointed rather than rounded at the top. The irreverent legend is that the confederates didn't want "no damn yankee" sitting on their headstones.

The headstones of the recipients of the Congressional Medal of Honor, the nation's highest award for valor, are also different. The names and other lettering are in gold and the design of the medal is embossed in the marble.

The bodies of 44 non-Americans are buried in Arlington—British, Canadians, South Africans, Chinese, French, Greeks and Dutch. There are also one German and two Italian prisoners of war. The Canadian Cross of Sacrifice was placed in Arlington by that government to honor all the Americans who served in Canada's armed forces during World Wars I and II.

General Abner Doubleday is buried in Arlington. He is known throughout the world as the man who codified the rules for the game of baseball, which some people think he invented. As another foonote in his history, Doubleday also fired the first union gun from Fort Sumter against the confederates at Charleston, South Carolina, in the initial engagement that began the Civil War.

Ironically, four men involved in pioneer air and space flights are buried near each other. Lt. Thomas Selfridge was the first person killed in a military plane crash. He was on a test flight in 1908 with Orville Wright at Fort Myer when the accident occurred. About 100 yards from the grave of Lt. Selfridge are the graves of the first two astronauts killed in the line of duty in the American space program, Lieutenant Commander Roger B. Chaffee and Lieutenant Colonel Virgil I. Grissom. And, not too far away, is the grave of Francis Gary Powers, the pilot of the advanced U-2 reconnaissance plane that was shot down over Russia. His capture aborted a summit meeting between President Dwight D. Eisenhower and Soviet Premier Nikita Khrushchev.

One of the loveliest memorials in Arlington is for Jane A. Delano. The marble statue of a serene woman honors Delano and the hundreds of other nurses who served in the American armed forces in World War I. The memorial is situated in the section of Arlington that is reserved as the final resting place of women who served as military nurses.

More than 185,000 persons are buried in Arlington National Cemetery. There are sections of infants; those missing in action; highly honored heroes and persons of achievement; and those who served quietly and competently in the growth and defense of the nation. There are men and women, white and black and red and brown and yellow. They are individuals whose lives and services collectively tell the story of America.

☞ *Paderewski*

Within a few yards of the blinding-white marble amphitheater at the Arlington National Cemetery stands the mast of the battleship *Maine*. Its sinking in Havana harbor on February 15, 1898 helped precipitate the war with Spain. Around the mast's marble base are the graves of seamen who lost their lives in the incident.

The base itself tells a poignant story.

Ignace Jan Paderewski was a great composer and pianist and a leading Polish statesman. He helped organize the provisional government for a free Poland in 1919 after the devastation of World War I, and later served as that nation's premier and foreign minister.

At the outbreak of World War II Poland was quickly overrun by Germany and the Soviet Union. With his country controlled by foreign armies, Paderewski became president of the Polish government in exile. He died in New York City in June 1941. Because his body could not be returned to his native land for burial, President Franklin Delano Roosevelt ordered that he would rest in Arlington Cemetery and be returned to his homeland when Poland was free.

To this day the body of Ignace Jan Paderewski rests in its sturdy oak coffin in the little crypt in the marble base of the memorial of the battleship *Maine*.

Poland is not yet free.

☞ *Oak Hill Cemetery*

In 1848 Washington's premier merchant, banker and philanthropist, W. W. Corcoran, bought a small tract of land at the top of the long hill rising from the Potomac that is Georgetown. There Corcoran established a cemetery, Oak Hill, supported by a trust fund. In the grove of huge oak trees are more than 17,000 graves of people who are closely identified with Georgetown and Washington. The famous and not so famous lie side by side.

Peggy O'Neale Eaton is buried in Oak Hill. She was a Georgetown tavern keeper's daughter whose marriage to President Andrew Jackson's secretary of war precipitated a crisis in Washington society that split the President's cabinet. Fussy dowagers wouldn't accept her because of her father's business, but Jackson insisted upon including her and her husband in polite society.

A poignant Oak Hill story centers around President Abraham Lincoln and his son Willie. The youngster, possibly Lincoln's favorite, died in the White

House in the middle of the President's term in office. The Lincoln family had no burial plot in Washington, so William Carroll, clerk of the Supreme Court, offered to place the child in Carroll's family's mausoleum in Oak Hill. There Willie was laid to rest until he could be moved to Illinois. The grief-stricken President often drove to Oak Hill, went to the crypt in the hillside of the cemetery and, sitting in a wrought iron chair, meditated for hours over the body of his young son.

The grave of John Howard Payne calls up a story of confusion and embarrassment. Payne, an actor, theater manager and sometime author, gained immortality for a single song he wrote for an obscure play, *The Maid of Milan*. The song was called *Home Sweet Home*. W. W. Corcoran, Oak Hill's founder, knew Payne slightly and admired the song he wrote. Payne died while serving as U.S. Consul in Tunis and was buried there. In 1883, 31 years later, Corcoran arranged to have the body exhumed and brought to Washington for reburial in Oak Hill.

It was a most elaborate occasion. Payne's body lay in state overnight in the old Corcoran Gallery (now the Renwick Gallery). The next morning the funeral procession wound its way from 17th Street and Pennsylvania Avenue to the cemetery. The procession was led by President Chester Arthur, Chief Justice Morrison R. Waite, General William Tecumsah Sherman and others. Corcoran had commissioned a one-and-one-half times life-size bust of the author to place on a pedestal over the grave.

Within days after the impressive ceremony, the rumor flew through Georgetown that Payne's bust portrayed him with a beard when everyone knew he was clean shaven. An Oak Hill trustee heard the rumor and quickly hired a stonemason to act as a barber and, with chisel and hammer, shave off the beard. The stonemason left the moustache.

Soon after that the Mathew Brady photograph of Payne that had been used on the invitation to the reinterment ceremony was closely examined. It showed, without question, that the honored songwriter did, indeed, have a full beard under his chin and part way up his cheek.

But it was too late. The stonemason-barber had done his work well, and the bust of Payne showed a smoothly shaven face. Oak Hill trustees were faced with two alternatives: order a new, bearded bust made, or leave it alone and hope that over the years people would forget that Payne had a beard. They left it alone.

☞ *Rock Creek Cemetery*

Just north of the Soldiers' and Airmen's Home on Rock Creek Church Road is the oldest church in the District—St. Paul's, built in 1712—and the oldest cemetery—Rock Creek, dedicated in 1719. Rock Creek Cemetery contains the graves of many eminent persons in American history.

Its most famous memorial is to Mrs. Henry Adams, wife of the author and historian who was grandson and great-grandson of two presidents of the United States. The seated, hooded, bronze figure is the acknowledged masterpiece of sculptor Augustus Saint-Gaudens. It has no formal title. The sculptor referred to it as "The Peace of God" and "The Mystery of the Hereafter." It has been incorrectly called "Grief" because Mark Twain remarked that the enigmatic figure embodied all human grief. (Twain wrote to his old friend Henry Adams about the memorial and asked what it meant. Adams replied, "Any 12-year-old knows what it means.")

There is one report that many years ago a Japanese admiral, knowing of Adams's interest in the orient, went to see the Saint-Gaudens sculpture. The admiral took one look and turned away in silent fury. He did not explain his reaction to his American friends who had accompanied him to the cemetery.

Each person who views the sculpture draws his or her own interpretation and reacts differently. It cannot be universally described.

☞ Glenwood Cemetery

Glenwood Cemetery is located in northeast Washington just south of The Catholic University of America. It was dedicated in 1854 and is the fourth oldest major cemetery in Washington, D.C. Originally, Glenwood consisted of some 90 acres, but over the years about 38 acres were sold to form part of the campus of Trinity College.

In one enclosed grave lies the body of a rather flamboyant Italian immigrant artist who spent nearly all his life painting the murals and frescoes on the walls of the Capitol building—Constantino Brumidi.

The cemetery also contains a disquieting marble statue of a child in a frilly, early 20th-century dress sitting in a tiny rocking chair. She was Teresina Vasco, who, according to cemetery records, died from burns received while playing with matches.

Perhaps the most imposing memorial in Glenwood honors Benjamin C. Grenup. He was a volunteer fireman who was killed in the line of duty while pulling, by hand, with other firemen, a heavy piece of firefighting equipment down Capitol Hill. Grenup tripped and was crushed to death by the wheels of the fire engine. His was the first recorded death of a fireman in the District of Columbia. The carvings on the sides of the base of his memorial portray the tools of firefighting and realistically depict the accident that killed him.

☞ *Battleground National Cemetery*

The smallest national cemetery in the United States is located at 6625 Georgia Avenue, N.W. Called Battleground National Cemetery, the one-acre plot holds the bodies of 41 union soldiers who died in the defense of Washington on July 12, 1864 at the battle of Fort Stevens.

The Civil War fort, partially restored, is just a half mile southwest of the cemetery. The attack, which was the only major assault on Washington during the Civil War, was carried out by General Jubal Early and his confederate force of about 8,000 men. It was repulsed by veterans of Wrights' Sixth Corps who had been sent from the battlefields around Richmond to save the capital.

It was during this engagement at Fort Stevens that a president of the United States, for the first time in history, came under enemy fire. President Lincoln had ridden out to the fort to watch the engagement. He was standing on a parapet when an officer five feet from him was wounded. The legend is that a young officer, Lt. Oliver Wendell Holmes, Jr., later a Supreme Court justice, shouted to the President, "Get down you fool, you'll get shot." The more likely story is that a senior union officer told President Lincoln that he would have to take cover or be removed from his position.

☞ *Mount Olivet Cemetery*

A city ordinance of 1852 prohibited interments within the city limits. At that time the city of Washington was contained within what is now Florida Avenue, then called Boundary Street. All the rest of the federal enclave was the District of Columbia. As the city grew outward into rural farmland from its original boundary it became Washington, D.C.

In 1858 the Roman Catholics of the city purchased Fenwick Farm on historic Bladensburg Road opposite the National Arboretum. The 75-acre tract of land was named Mount Olivet Cemetery and the dead of all the Catholic cemeteries were moved to this single large burial ground.

Here are buried James Hoban, designer of the White House, and many other notables of the military and naval services who died before Arlington National Cemetery was opened.

And, in Mount Olivet, almost completely hidden by shrubbery is a small stone bearing simply the name "Mrs. Surratt." She was the woman hanged for alleged conspiracy in the assassination of President Lincoln.

☞ *Congressional Cemetery*

Statesmen, Indian chiefs, musicians, victims of tragic accidents, the forgotten son of a first lady and even one of those who plotted the assassination of a president are all gathered together in one place in Washington—in Congressional Cemetery. Established as a small private cemetery in 1807, Congressional was taken over by Christ Episcopal Church in 1812. In 1816 a Congressional committee selected one section as a place to inter members of Congress. Today 19 senators and 43 representatives are buried there.

• Among those who held elective office now buried in the cemetery is Elbridge Gerry, who died as vice president of the United States in 1814. He had a long and distinguished career as a patriot and statesman, was very active in the second Continental Congress and was a signer of the Declaration of Independence. Gerry was elected Governor of Massachusetts in 1810. An action by him while serving in that office assured his permanent place in history.

The state legislature passed a redistricting bill approved by Gerry. Political opponents studying the new map commented that one district was so contorted that it looked like a salamander. Another observer quipped, "That's not a salamander, that's a gerrymander."

Thus was born a political term that has endured to this day.

• A solemn young lady about the age of ten named Marion Kahlert stands in her victorian dress gazing forever straight ahead. She was the first victim of an automobile accident in the District in 1904.

• A very modest headstone marks the grave of John Payne Todd. He was the son of the vivacious Dolley Madison by her first marriage. She was later the wife of the fourth president.

• John Philip Sousa, the March King, and J. Edgar Hoover, the FBI chieftain, are also buried in Congressional.

• Twenty-one women killed in an explosion and fire at the Washington Arsenal in 1864 are buried in a mass grave under a 20-foot high marble shaft.

• Under one of the cenotaphs is the body of the Choctaw Indian chief Push-ma-ta-ha. He was the chief who brought his braves to help General Andrew Jackson fight the Spanish in the Pensacola campaign. The small-scale war began in 1817 when two British adventurers convinced the Creek Indians in the Pensacola area that they had been robbed during the War of 1812. The Creeks went on the warpath and Jackson was ordered to punish them. He routed their forces, hanged their chiefs, court-martialed the two British adventurers, captured Pensacola, where he ousted the Spanish governor, and claimed the territory for the United States. England, Spain and the Congress were furious but the peace was kept.

The upshot was that Spain sold Florida to the United States and Jackson became a new force in political America.

Later Push-ma-ta-ha came to Washington to help negotiate a treaty. Of course, he called on his old friend and companion in arms Andrew Jackson, then a senator from Tennessee. The legend is that the two of them went out to celebrate their reunion and didn't make it back to their respective boarding houses, but slept in the open in a park on a bitter winter night. The Choctaw chief became ill and several days later died. His last words were—and they are on the cenotaph— "let the big guns boom over me." Senator Jackson complied, and Push-ma-ta-ha was buried with full military honors and plenty of artillery salutes by the United States Army.

☞ *Mt. Zion Cemetery*

Behind a mundane low-rise apartment building at 27th and Q Streets, N.W., is one of Washington's oldest historic sites marking the black presence in the city. It is Mt. Zion Cemetery.

The cemetery's story began when the first Georgetown Methodist Society, now known as Dumbarton United Methodist Church, was officially recognized in 1772. In 1808 the Georgetown Society acquired a piece of land along Rock

Creek as a burial place for its members, their slaves and the freed black persons who were members of the congregation.

In 1816 the "coloured brethren" of the Georgetown Society formed a separate congregation known today as the Mt. Zion United Methodist Church. It was the first black church in Washington. Later, in 1842, a group of free black women formed the Female Union Band Society and purchased land adjacent to the old Methodist cemetery for a burial ground.

Today the two parcels of land, amounting to about three acres, cannot be told apart. Together they are known as the Mt. Zion Cemetery. The entire plot is in disarray.

The old burial vault on the grounds, reportedly, was a way station on the underground railway. Some slaves fleeing to freedom who died along the way lie in unmarked graves on the hillside.

On one side of the cemetery is a low rise in the land. According to legend it is a mass grave of German mercenaries who were killed or died in the British capture of Washington in 1814.

☞ *Female Stranger*

Alexandria has several fascinating and historic cemeteries. One of the most important is the graveyard of Christ Church, which contains some of the ear-

liest sculptured gravestones in the area. The church itself was attended frequently by George Washington, and General Robert E. Lee was also a member.

Perhaps the most intriguing single grave in Alexandria is in the cemetery plot of St. Paul's Church. There a flat, marble marker carries the epitaph of the "Female Stranger," who died October 14, 1816, aged 23 years and 8 months.

No one really knows who the "Female Stranger" was, nor why she is buried at St. Paul's, but many versions of her story of mystery, violence, passion and devotion exist.

The generally accepted legend, with variations, is that the "Female Stranger" was the ward of a distinguished well-to-do English gentleman. As she grew from childhood and became a beautiful young woman, the guardian, who had become elderly, fell in love with her. He willed his large estate to her and told her of his love and his desire to marry her. She was horrified at the prospect of marriage to one she regarded as a father; besides, she was in love with another. When her fiancé came calling a few days later he was accosted by the elderly gentleman. An argument ensued; the guardian fell off a step, hit his head and died almost at once.

The young couple was terrified and, feeling their story would not be believed, fled England for America after a hasty wedding.

At this point the versions of the story begin to vary wildly.

The more romantic version is that the couple disembarked the ship from England at Alexandria because the "Female Stranger" had taken sick. They took rooms at Gadsby's Tavern where, in spite of medical attention, she died.

But, before she died, the "Female Stranger" exacted a promise from her husband that he would not put her name on a headstone because it might lead to his arrest for murder. He complied, and she was buried in St. Paul's as "The Female Stranger." Shortly after, the man changed his name and found employment in New York. There he was accused of embezzlement and served a prison term.

Years later, disconsolate, he returned to Virginia to be near the grave of his young bride. Because he had no resources he went into the wilderness near the Little Falls of the Potomac and built a cabin. He became known as a hermit named John, and would often row down the Potomac to place flowers on the grave of the "Female Stranger."

About 1850, broken in body and spirit, John wrote his brother in England and asked that he visit him. The letter was delayed, and not until a year later did the brother find John's cabin. It was empty except for a note requesting that John be buried at night, secretly, in the grave of his wife, "The Female Stranger." In the woods nearby the brother found John's skeleton.

Two nights later the brother rowed down the river to Alexandria and buried John's body with the "Female Stranger" in St. Paul's Cemetery.

A romantic mystery does not require indisputable facts to make it fascinating.

Postscript

When a book like this is finished one feels that, no matter how thoroughly or carefully any of its subjects has been explored, there is much more to be found about them and other people and events in the rich lode of Washington history.

Such a book actually becomes a challenge to the reader or buff to do his own exploration. If you care to share your findings, let me hear from you and perhaps we can produce another volume of *Footnote Washington* sometime in the future.

Thank you.

BR

Acknowledgments

It is impossible to acknowledge all the help I received from many people and the shelves of publications that, in one way or another, contributed to this book.

The list of references that aided me begins with the two incomparable works of James M. Goode, curator of the Smithsonian Castle, *The Outdoor Sculpture of Washington, D.C.* and *Capital Losses;* the WPA Guide to the Nation's Capitol; Constance McLaughlin Green's *Washington; Carp's Washington;* the publications of the White House and U.S. Capitol Historical Societies; the Columbia Historical Society and those of the nearby counties and cities; the Washington section of the D.C. Public Library and the Peabody Room in the Georgetown Branch; and the libraries of the cities and counties in the Washington area.

Information about places and things in Washington or elsewhere is impossible to acquire without consulting the experts of the U.S. Park Service. There are many of them and they are most generous and patient. This is true also of the experts at the Library of Congress and the Archives.

Individuals who assisted me are Florian Thayne of the U.S. Capitol's Architect's Office; Fred Schwengel, president of the U.S. Capitol Historical Society;

Betty Monkman of the White House Curator's Office; Perry Fisher and William Press of the Columbia Historical Society; Josh Billings, Civil War historian; Bob Truax, photograph and print collector; Nan Montgomery of the Washington Cathedral; my close friend Charles Kelly; and, of course, EPM editor Pamela Noda.

I have started something I knew I never should have begun—naming organizations and individuals who helped with this effort. It is not possible to name them all, so I will stop with a heartfelt "thanks." They know who they are, and they know I mean it.

Last, though perhaps this acknowledgment should be first, I thank my immediate family: Julie, my wife, who for years urged me to get something down on paper rather than radio and television scripts or tapes; our daughters, Brennan, an expert "dunner" whose talent as an editor is evident in the text; and Julianne, who, in every phone conversation from her succession of homes with her doctor husband in Dallas, San Diego and Dickinson, North Dakota, asked how the book was coming.

I couldn't ignore that kind of pressure from three determined women.

Thank you.